Revenge
of the
Latchkey
Kids

An Illustrated Guide
to Surviving the 90s and Beyond

By Ted Rall

WORKMAN PUBLISHING · NEW YORK

Published simultaneously in Canada by Thomas Allen & Son Limited.

Library of Congress Cataloging-in-Publication Data

Rall, Ted
Revenge of the latchkey kids: an illustrated survival guide to the 90s and beyond/by Ted Rall.
p.   cm.
ISBN 0-7611-1040-2(hc).—ISBN 0-7611-0745-2(pbk)
1. American wit and humor.   I. Title
PN6182.R276 1998
741.5'973–dc21   97-40927
                                        CIP

Some of the chapters in this book previously appeared elsewhere, in slightly different form: "College Is for Suckers," "Slack Off for a Better America," and "A Sprocket in Satan's Bulldozer" were published in *Might* Magazine. "The Sporting Life" was published in *Maximumrocknroll*.
"Life Sentence" lyrics by Jello Biafra, reprinted by permission of Decay Music © 1982, courtesy of Alternative Tentacles Records.
"Dead End" lyrics by East Bay Ray, reprinted by permission of Decay Music, © 1982, courtesy of Alternative Tentacles Records.
Excerpt from "The Simpsons" courtesy of Matt Groening, Twentieth Century Fox Film Corporation. All rights reserved.

I could never have written this book without the support of the following people. Mega-ultra-humble big-time thanks to Jello Biafra, Alice Chang, Stuart Dodds, Dave Eggers, Simson Garfinkel, Susan Grode, Matt Groening, Dan Hassan, Julie Just, Anne Kostick, Jon Landman, Toni Mendez, Susan Peters, Sue Roush, Lee Salem, Cole Smithey, Valerie Vineyard, Peter Workman, and Tim Yohannan.

Ted Rall sings Uzbek folk songs in a high, squeaky voice at weddings, becomes disturbingly excited while watching those Sunday morning talking-head shows, and occasionally gets cereal stuck under his gum line. If you require these services, please write: Ted Rall, c/o Universal Press Syndicate, 4520 Main Street, Kansas City, MO 64111

Workman Publishing Company, Inc.
708 Broadway
New York, NY 10003-9555

Manufactured in the United States of America
First printing March 1998
10 9 8 7 6 5 4 3 2 1

Cover and interior design by Janet Vicario.

DEDICATION

This book is dedicated to my mom, Yvonne Touzet-Rall. She taught me to question basic assumptions, never to settle for second-best. She put up with more nonsense than any human being should have to tolerate. And she did it alone.

It is also dedicated to my wife, Judy S. Chang, for the many hundreds of hours she spent reading, discussing, and editing it, not to mention inspiring its contents and forgiving my monopolization of the computer.

CONTENTS

INTRODUCTION

by Jules Feiffer

First, get it out of your head that this is your typical political-cartoon collection. That is not what Ted Rall has in mind. There are cartoons, about 200 of them, but what Ted Rall is most interested in collecting here are his thoughts. On everything. A spicy stew of high-handed judgments—part drawing, part essay, part memoir-confession, part tantrum.

The text is the thing. Funny, fractious here and there, nasty now and then, brilliant. The cartoons come on as sidebars (or side-men, playing sassy-satiric riffs off the text). They are vital, but secondary.

Ted Rall is a Gen-Xer, and not at all happy about it. He draws and writes for his fellow Gen-Xers, whom he judges harshly. According to Ted, they don't care about much, and remember next to nothing. This makes Ted a bad generational fit. A student of history, economics, and math, he knows where we've been, sees where we're headed, and sums it up as disastrous.

His social criticism of Gen-Xers is scathing, but not without compassion. No such luck for members of the boomer generation that precedes him. For them, it's unwavering contempt.

Ted's view of the world comes out of an almost contemplative cynicism. It is reinforced by everything he sees around him. But it's a quirky kind of cynicism, in that it makes him more active, not passive. Rather than abandon the playing field because the game is fixed, he plays that much harder, certain that the results will be awful.

Over and over, he acts against his own sense of logic. There's a zany kind of courage to this that has to be admired.

My own time was less cynical. We who entered adulthood by way of the Cold War Fifties were full of hope and idealism. Inevitably, we lost our idealism, but if we were lucky, held onto our hope. Not that it ever gets us far. But it does get us through the day; not to be sneezed at in these times.

Ted Rall is an abandoned son. And that appears to be the most significant event in his life, from age three to the present. His father, "A high-ranking Air Force civilian," met his mother at NATO headquarters in Paris in 1961. "He brought her to Chicago," Ted writes, "married her, and had me in '63. By '66 he was history."

Hardly. Unless it's living history that he's talking about. I doubt if there's a moment in Ted Rall's life, past or present, whether its his art, his on-again, off-again jobs, his on-again, off-again sex life, his politics and anti-politics, that's not forever stage-managed by what his father did to him at three, and, for good measure, did again when he was nineteen.

"I've always had an attitude," Ted Rall writes. And elsewhere: "I . . . enjoy a remarkable ability to remember the way things were and to hold grudges."

His achievement is to translate his grudges into work, and work into a social vision. It's not easy. He is so pissed off, by so many more things than a reader can readily handle, that, one fears, early on, he's out of control.

But, if in the beginning, his tone strikes us as excessive, by the end of his argument (and this book is an argument), we are forced to concede that his rage is a more appropriate response to how we Americans live out our lives today, than the more mature, balanced outlook which is, of course, denial and compliance.

Ted Rall, now in his thirties, is by some quirk of generational fate, trapped in permanent adolescence. You may find him to be self-pitying, irritating, endlessly self-involved, but—like many adolescents—Ted is able to spot the hyperbole and hypocracies of his elders with a clear eye and perfect pitch.

There are some great quotes in this book, and thoughts every bit as compelling as the quotes.

I am left to conclude that he is the only kind of revolutionary that one can take seriously after the '60s: The one-on-one, freelance revolutionary, who exepcts to get nowhere, and works hard to achieve that goal.

Which may be a good thing. With a little power, Ted Rall would be absolutely terrifying. Still . . . what remains of the old lefty in me kind of has to hope.

I. NEUROCHEMICAL WARFARE

"If Ted doesn't stop fighting with his classmates, he will be kicked off the bus."
—*My first-grade report card, 1969*

've always had an attitude. Back in the third grade, I remember my teacher explaining that, even though it appears throughout such classic works of fiction as the Bible, "damn" was a bad word, inappropriate for public use, particularly in school. Afterward, I took to using the word in every single sentence, as in "Damn, may I please go to the damned rest room, dammit?" She sent me to the principal's office the first few times I did this, but eventually gave up, and I spent the entire year strolling the halls repeating the D-word thousands of times.

As one of the shortest kids in junior high, the juvenile pecking order made my imperative crystal clear: Stay inconspicuous; avoid harm. Instead, I repeatedly found myself sneaking up behind some teenage behemoth and kicking him as hard as possible in the shins while screaming insults concerning his mother's extracurricular sex habits. I fully expected—and received—a pounding each time. But I just couldn't help myself. It was worth getting my ass kicked just to see the look of surprise on the bullies' faces.

Moving to Manhattan to attend college helped calm me down a bit. The first time I observed New York motorists at a stop signal, revving their engines while watching for the green light going the other way to turn yellow before flooring the gas like racers at Le Mans, I knew I'd found home. Here was an entire city full of people just as full of nervous anxiety as me, and many of them were armed. Now to get rid of the goddamn tourists!

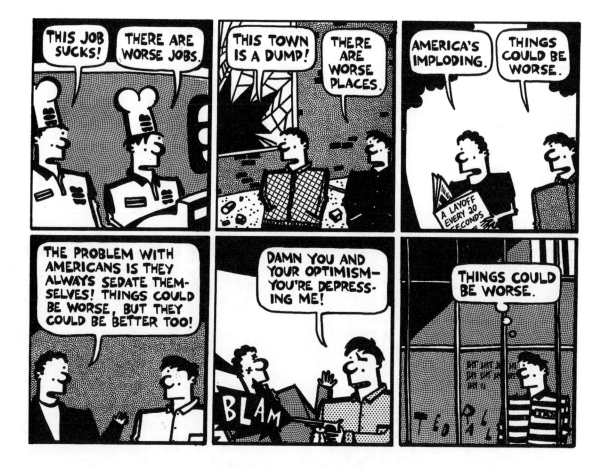

Recently, biochemists writing in the journal *Science* revealed that easily irritated, uptight people like me probably have a slightly shorter version of the gene that handles the movement of the neurochemical serotonin from one brain cell to the next. Antidepressant drugs like Prozac work by stemming the loss of serotonin, so having the shortened transporter gene acts like anti-Prozac, making a person nervous, grumpy, cynical, sometimes even neurotic. Pessimism, it turns out, may not be so much a personality trait as a genetic disorder.

The scientists studied over five hundred college students, most of them white males like me, and asked them whether they agreed or disagreed with such statements as "I am not a worrier" and "Frightening thoughts sometimes come into my head." They took blood samples, and they found that those students with truncated transporter genes tended to be more neurotic than those with the longer ones.

I am depressed about this. I have spent much of my life arguing with my optimistic counterparts in defense of my finely honed negative attitudes, and for the last few years, pessimism expressed through cartoons has kept me in beer money. For me, negativity isn't the default mode that results after abandoning positive thinking; it's simply the only

My enduring belief that everything sucks, based on scientific observation, conveniently explains such seemingly disparate phenomena as the continuing popularity of R.E.M., cigars, and the Republican Party. My negativity has been vindicated as I've watched my friends and colleagues suffer disappointment after disappointment when they were passed over for promotions, fired unfairly, and mistreated by their significant

logical course of action in a world where there's always someone with nothing better to do than to think up some new budget cut. I have taught myself to take for granted that all politicians eventually become corrupt, that all corporate executives enjoy polluting rivers, that most people are stark raving idiots. I've always found satisfaction in the predictability that my admittedly rancid worldview offered me.

others. The newspapers are choked with articles depicting people shocked by some negative turn of events like a draconian welfare-reform bill or a hurricane blowing their house out to sea.

Not me! I've accepted such catastrophes as being expelled from college and getting fired for a theft I didn't commit as a matter of course, the inevitable result of life's vicious unfairness in a world populated by morons, exploiters, liars, and opportunists.

Maybe I never put on a happy face or had a nice day and maybe frightening thoughts roamed around my frontal lobes, but my philosophy—that no matter how bad anything is, it can and probably will get worse—has always worked. That Reaganism bankrupted the Treasury and that the culture of divorce led to more teen suicides came as no surprise to me; nor will

time I went through a near-death experience, my might-have-been-last thought was: "It figures."

No one should confuse pessimism with lethargy or apathy. Just because you expect the worst doesn't mean that you stop fighting for a better world. Pessimism is not paralysis. The difference is, pessimists know that the struggle for a better tomorrow is a serious uphill battle.

the lost jobs caused by free trade or the incredible misery precipitated by Clinton's welfare reform or the cultural fallout wreaked by the aging of suburbia. Not every idea is worthwhile, and not every plan deserves to be tried out—after all, who didn't know beforehand that balancing the budget by cutting taxes was an act of lunacy? Pessimists are never disappointed, only pleasantly surprised when things go well. The last

Now I face a philosophical dilemma: If the nervous pessimism that worked so well in the past wasn't the result of an intelligent choice, as I used to believe, but rather a genetic mutation caused by my mom living too close to a nuclear power plant while she was pregnant, shouldn't I reconsider it? After all, one's behavior ought to be the culmination of one's experiences and the result of careful deliberation, not of some arbitrary biological factor.

But this, of course, leads to another question: Am I in fact free to become a giddy, toothy-grinned optimist? Or am I genetically doomed to my bad attitude?

Eventually I'll have myself tested to determine the truth about my atrocious outlook on life. Whatever I find, I'll take comfort from another result of that gene study: Nearly 70 percent of the human race possesses this pessimistic, anxiety-laden short gene. Dr. Una McCann of the National Institute of Mental Health told *The New York Times* that the popularity of genetically enforced pessimism could be the result of Darwinism: "Anxiety is there for a really good reason. It's one of the things that is part of our genes because it's protective." In other words, *pessimism is a higher state of evolution than optimism.*

Drink more coffee, have more arguments, suspect everyone—it just doesn't get any better than this!

2. TO HELL WITH FATHER'S DAY

*"I've practiced law in this state for more than 30 years. During that time,
I've never met anyone as pig-headed as your father."*

—My mom's divorce lawyer, 1968

The Great American Dad Disappearance began in the 1960s, and it's only getting worse. If you're under forty, your parents are probably divorced. You were likely raised by your mother, who probably received very little child support or alimony. Since women earn almost one-third less than men, your opportunities—going to college, for example—were drastically downsized.

Still, if you're the product of a divorce, or know someone who is, the last thing you should do is encourage the irresponsible behavior of the male elite. Fathers who abandon their families deserve nothing but contempt—and they certainly shouldn't be deemed to have "fathers' rights." I wholeheartedly recommend this brand of exorcism to anyone still burdened by a father who doesn't love them: Accept that your dad is damaged, and move on—in this shipwrecked society, it's every man for himself. You have to save yourself so that you can salvage what sanity you have left and become a viable parent yourself someday.

Without a doubt the worst damage caused by the Big D is that it puts your emotional life on hold. Children of divorce never accept what has happened to them. After all, nothing could be more unfair than to be born into an imploding family—as a country's social structure collapses, that's when kids

need an intact family the most. So I, like every other product of a broken home I know, spent years waiting for Dad to come to his senses and come home. And when it became clear that that wouldn't happen— his new wife probably wouldn't have approved—I waited for him to fulfill his minimal responsibilities as a father. After I gave up on that—when I went to college—I hoped that we might at least be friends. Respect was out of the question, but perhaps

our genetic codes shared enough similarities to permit us to throw back a few cold ones and watch Steve McQueen movies without me succumbing to the urge to murder him.

It took me until 1991 to give up on my dad. I was twenty-eight. He had bailed on me back during the Johnson administration, which demonstrates how quickly I catch on.

Although my nominal father hadn't written me a letter in ten years, I'd never written him off. I had always hoped that he

would realize what an asshole he'd been and would make the choice to reform himself, and that I would be able to forgive him afterward. The biological urge to keep an intact family was evidently stronger in me than it was in him, but children are a conservative nonvoting bloc. They crave stability to the point of boredom. In any event, I'd always thought that since I had only two parents, it was reasonable to tolerate a lot of nasty behavior to avoid losing one of them.

As I eventually learned, I'd only had one parent to begin with, but I had to learn that the hard way.

One day I mailed off a nine-page letter enumerating his crimes and what he could do, if anything, to redeem himself. I even included an invoice for my college tuition, adjusted for inflation, viewing his reaction to this retroactive billing as a litmus test of his good intentions. I sent it from a mailbox in front of a health-food store. It was a symbol, I felt, of my move to take charge of my own mental health.

THE COLUMBUS PEACE SUMMIT

A few weeks later, to my surprise, my father called me for the first time in more than a decade. He told me that he was sending me a plane ticket. He arranged for me to meet him in an Embassy Suites motel on the I-270 loop outside Columbus, Ohio—the kind with the rooms facing into a big atrium, with glass-walled elevators—for a weekend. It was standard behavior for him: anything to avoid the gritty reality of an actual city, anything to keep the game on his turf, within driving distance of his house.

He told me during the call that he was disturbed that I felt as I did and wanted to work things out, or at

least clear the air. I allowed that the air was in dire need of filtration. I figured that since perhaps he didn't have a clue what being a father was all about, he needed some pointers. I'd tell him what I needed from him, and if he chose to disregard my demands, so be it. He could no longer claim to be surprised or confused about my disgust.

It was without a doubt one of the most surreal experiences of my life. On a Friday afternoon, Dad picked me up at the Columbus airport in his Chevy Suburban—a far cry from the '73 Grand Prix he used to tool around town in—and drove us straight to the motel. I wouldn't see the sun again until Sunday.

Our Columbus Peace Summit was two days of the pure hell that can be experienced only by people who share not one single idea of how human beings should interact. Dad went to sleep at 9:00 P.M., as was his habit, and arose at 5:30 A.M. to watch ESPN. Out of respect for the proceedings, I awoke both days at 9:00 to face marathon sessions of noncommunication.

It was all very civil. Neither one of us ever lost his temper; no tears were shed. I reiterated my litany of complaints, and at every turn he refuted them with one of the following two explanations:

1. His parents, though they had been financially generous, were cold and insensitive Missouri Lutherans. Because he had never experienced any emotions whatsoever, he couldn't empathize with other people's pain. Therefore, he had no choice but to let my mom and me starve while he soothed himself with new stereo equipment.

2. Like the father in Johnny Cash's "A Boy Named Sue," the man who never used my name—he always called me "son"—asserted that his behavior was designed to make me stronger so I wouldn't, as he expressed it, wear my heart on my sleeve. Emotions kill.

Finally, despite inadequate sleep and fresh air, I enjoyed a mental awakening, the glorious brain clearing that hits you like a second cup of coffee. I finally knew that two points were preventing a resolution to my fucked-up relationship with my dad. First, he'd never loved me—I'd just been too stupid and naive to see that. Second:

"Dad," I asked softly, "would you say that you've ever done anything wrong?"

"What do you mean?" He squinted at me suspiciously.

"I mean, have you ever made a mistake?"

"When? What mistake?"

"In general—have you ever made a mistake of any kind during the course of your life? Do you have any regrets, any wish that you'd done something differently?"

He thought about that for a few moments, which was astonishing enough. Then he said no.

And that was that. Like the federal building coming down in a tiny Oklahoma City inside my chest cavity, I felt all the thought and pain and angst I'd suffered over my dad collapse. I knew at that moment that I had spent my entire life fretting and worrying about someone who was completely out of his mind.

On Sunday he drove off in his Suburban, smugly satisfied that he had set me straight. He promised to visit me in New York and said that he felt great that we had had such a productive conference. Like Chamberlain leaving Munich, he didn't know that in my eyes he'd just killed himself.

I flew back to New York minus a father. It felt like excising a tumor: painful but a real relief. Now I appreciate my mom much more, not the least for surviving a marriage to this creep and for doing double duty as a parent. I stopped chasing after my dad simply because he contributed some sperm to the reproductive process.

Parenthood is a privilege; the millions of parents, mostly fathers, who walk away from

their kids every year are the real losers. They're the sorriest bunch of human beings in our society—overgrown children who are so irresponsible and worthless that they can't even fulfill the primordial, instinctual imperative to raise offspring. By never experiencing parenthood, they never mature as adults.

The single parents who remain behind to raise the kids are the heroes of America after the sexual revolution, the crack troops in the war against familial disintegration. Raising children on limited funds, without enough free time, is a nearly impossible task to which millions of women (and a few men) rise every day. The government is beginning to crack down on deadbeat dads by increasing child-support payments and chasing fugitive fathers across state lines, but their efforts are inadequate. As a society,

we need to deluge one-parent families with economic assistance in the form of college grants, free medical care, and paid time off from work. As individuals, we should reach out to help these families in any way we can. But most of all, single parents deserve to know that their children appreciate them, a statement most effectively made by the wholesale physical and emotional rejection of an absentee parent. Cut off these useless appendages as soon as you possibly can—it's the only effective method of exorcizing the demon of divorce.

THE CASE FOR ONE LESS GREETING-CARD HOLIDAY

My dad knows better than to root around in his mailbox as the third Sunday in June approaches. He won't find a card from me. It's been at least a decade since I dropped two bucks to show that I care enough to send the very best.

The cliché of father-son tension is the stuff of Hemingway stories, James Dean flicks, Johnny Cash songs, and Sunday newspaper magazine spreads. There's nothing new about kids failing to appreciate their dads until they flat-line under the oxygen tent. Nowadays, however, the rifts that separate American fathers from their children are far more serious than big band versus rock music, bigotry versus tolerance, or three-piece suits versus long hair. Now it's all about responsibility and abdication.

My dad, a high-ranking Air Force civilian, met my mom, then an office worker at the Paris-based NATO office, in 1961. He brought her to Chicago and married her, and they had me in '63. By '66, he was history.

The years that followed are amply documented in the files of the county clerk's office: court dates for failure to remit child support on time and the various medical bills he'd agreed to pay under the divorce decree; disputes over visitation (alternating Saturdays and Sundays, 1:00 P.M. to 7:00 P.M., plus two weeks straight during August); and his successful machinations to slither out of paying college tuition.

Like many American men, my father believed that he had divorced me along with his wife. As my mom and I struggled to survive on her four-figure starting teacher's salary, Dad lived the dream, moving first into a swank bachelor's pad and later into the refrigerator-white suburbs south of Dayton, buying a new car annually and buying a new split-level house. When he ran out of new consumer goods to buy, he remarried.

Dad's willingness to let my mom and me starve to death was undoubtedly sufficient justification to never to speak to him again. But in the end it was his vicious insults ("If your cartoons were any good, you'd get paid more for them") and self-justifications ("I've never experienced any emotions") that prompted me to quit answering his newsy letters about nothing. Opting not to invite him to my wedding closed the deal: He's outta here.

Most divorced men have almost nothing to do with the upbringing of their children. In her classic twenty-year study of divorcing upper-middle-class families, San Francisco psychologist Judith S. Wallerstein found that only one father out of the 150 families she studied provided

more financial support to his children than the amount ordered by the family court. The majority didn't even pay that much, although all the dads in the study held high-paying jobs. Perhaps more disturbing than their astonishing cheapness was the revelation that they spent little to no time with their children. By the time their former tax deductions became teenagers, the vast majority of ex-fathers had stopped visiting them.

And spare me the letters from you model divorced dads who got screwed in family court, adore your kids, and are denied visitation rights by your vindictive, greedy ex-wives. Like men raped by women, there aren't enough of you in the whole country to fill a phone booth.

Surprisingly, the issue of disappearing dads rarely comes up in public discourse about the decline of the family and the alienation of young adults. When it does, it's usually to attack "deadbeat dads" (as if paying child support fulfilled all of a divorced father's responsibilities) or to bash African-American men for abandoning their kids—this, despite the fact that whites do it just as often as blacks and can usually afford the extra expense. Maybe it's because the right-wing politicians who exploit the issue of family values—people like Ronald Reagan and Bob Dole—were themselves classic examples of rich white men who dumped their first wives and kids. One of the most enduring images of the early 1980s was a photo that appeared on the front page of the *New York Post* of Ron Reagan Jr., filing for unemployment benefits while his dad was busy sinking the country into debt and smuggling coke to fund the contras.

The effects of divorce on children are

fairly straightforward. As kids, divorce victims are more likely to suffer from malnutrition and disease. As teens, they're more likely to get depressed and commit suicide. As adults, their perception that the future is uncertain causes them to avoid commitments, both personal and professional. They earn and save less and get in trouble with the law more. They have difficulty holding jobs.

President Clinton became the first American politician to publicly address divorce itself as a problem. I was sitting with the Michigan delegation at Madison Square Garden when he accepted his party's nomination at the 1992 Democratic National Convention. He addressed children of divorce: "I am one of you. You will finally be heard." When I looked around, I saw that almost everyone under forty was sobbing.

I don't know what happened to that promise. Perhaps Clinton figured that you can't legislate fatherhood. But he could persuade colleges not to consider an absentee father's income when evaluating a student's financial-aid needs. He could propose tax credits for divorced mothers and force fathers to pay back child support, plus interest penalties (even if the unpaid amount dates back decades). But before he does any of that, he should issue a proclamation deleting Father's Day from the place it currently occupies on the third Sunday of June.

Now that most of us don't have fathers anymore, it makes no more sense to celebrate dads than to devote days to haberdashers, stonemasons, or any other relic of a long-dead past. Moreover, perpetuating the Father's Day tradition is insulting and offensive to the vast majority of American children and the mothers who raise them alone.

If dads ever begin parenting in significant numbers in the future, we could consider reestablishing Father's Day, but in the meantime, there's no reason to go on pretending that they're doing a stellar job.

Besides, you can always deduct those two bucks a year you save on the card from your dad's way-overdue child support.

3. CHOOSING YOUR CHILDHOOD

"Society is a carnivorous flower."
—*Graffiti on Sunoco Station, Dayton, Ohio, 1976*

Even people who haven't yet been born know that their personalities will be fully formed by the age of five. Did you throw your Hot Wheels around when you were three? If so, look out—you're doomed to become a drunk driver, kill a busload of born-again Christians, walk away from the smoldering wreckage unscathed, and face a six-month suspended driving permit.

RESEARCHERS BELIEVE THE LAST 2 MONTHS OF PREGNANCY ARE BIOLOGICALLY UNNECESSARY... THEY'RE ONLY TO MAKE BABIES CUTE, SO PARENTS WILL WANT TO TAKE CARE OF THEM.
NOW LOOK FOR THESE NEW EVOLUTIONARY INNOVATIONS TO KEEP MODERN PARENTS AROUND...

Pop psychology exists in numerous forms—$150-an-hour shrinks, self-help books, talk-radio shows—it's one huge, multibillion-dollar business. And that's not even including the untold hundreds of millions that pour each year into pharmaceutical companies manufacturing such synthetic peace of mind as Zoloft and Prozac. All of this mental misery can be traced back to Mom and Dad—and that

treason is repackaged as "free trade," missiles are called "peacekeepers," and avoiding doctors is called "alternative medicine," isn't it time that the advertising industry's cultural dung be put to good use?

The past is constantly being revisited and reinvented. The same government that openly dispatched Japanese-Americans to concentration camps during World War II issues checks and apologies to the victims.

Christmas they gave you a Scrabble set instead of a Shetland pony. Today we have a new generation with a new set of psychological problems, typically caused by disappearing dads and working moms. However, the basic premise remains the same as it did when Freud invented all this angst stuff: Your childhood messed you up.

In this age of spin and bluster, in which

Vacuous musical abominations like Kansas and AC/DC are regurgitated as '70s classics. Now is the time for all good victims to come to the aid of their own sorry selves—by reinventing their childhoods!

If experiences common to an entire nation can be changed via historical revisionism, it ought to be comparatively easy to recast your own psychological demons the same way. For instance, let's say that you'd forgotten that an uncle had molested you when you were seven years old (repressed memory of sexual abuse is a standard psychological dilemma facing American adults) and that you now find yourself discussing what happened on national daytime talk shows, some of which are poorly rated. You remembered this traumatic event only because you watched the Reds lose to

pened, and may have, in fact, *never* happened, unless it did, but in any case you've now forgotten it again anyway. Got that?

In any event, the first step toward reconstituting your upbringing is to identify your current perception of your childhood (since no one can check up on your story, you're free to say anything you want). Best of all, the more often you repeat the story of your "new" childhood, the more

the Pirates, and the same thing happened back in 1970, when you were watching the game on TV in the family room and he touched you in the dirty place.

You could eliminate all this by obtaining a video of a game between the same two teams, but with the opposite outcome, logically causing you to once again *forget* the repressed memory, which now never hap-

you'll actually believe it yourself—*which makes it true!*

Using statistics, metaphysics, and a background in civil engineering, it is now possible to choose the past that works for *you*—thanks to this low-tech, *Cosmo*-style test.

Select the family background archetype with which you most closely identify:

Generic Dysfunctional: 80 percent of Americans suffer from family dysfunctionality, wherein parents, siblings, and/or relatives in the extended family (aunts, uncles, etc.) did not act "normal." Dysfunctionality encompasses a wide range of such inappropriate behaviors as alcoholism, sexual perversion, violence, favoritism, and obsession with *Mannix* and *Columbo* reruns. *If you came from a dysfunctional family, give yourself 8 points.*

Garden-Variety Psychotic: 15 percent of Americans have parents who are serial killers, politicians, or both. When they tell their friends "you'll never understand," they mean it. They had severed heads in the freezer, torsos in the root cellar, and *MacNeil-Lehrer* on the tube. *If you're from a psychotic family, give yourself 11 points.*

Standard-Issue Normal: Children from "normal" families come from intact two-parent households in which the mother and father loved each other and put their children first, supporting them both financially and emotionally. Normal families used discipline but not abuse, drove station wagons with fake wood paneling, decorated their house with colonial furniture from Ethan Allen, and never, ever, owned a Leonard Nimoy record without understanding the irony involved. The number of normal families is widely considered to be statistically insignificant. *If your childhood was normal, give yourself 2 points.*

Military: Dad had a buzz cut, mom kept a stack of change-of-address cards handy, and you changed schools more often than you showered. *If you were an army brat, give yourself 14 points.*

The next step is to determine which of the following commonly accepted self-images you would like to project to other people. Please select one of the following choices (two if you'd like to blend) of how you would like to be perceived:

Pathetic Whiner: This image will allow you to gain sympathy and to write collections of repressed little stories that sell fairly well, but it's best if you're a twenty-year-old folk-rock singer from southern Illinois. Disadvantage: You'll have lots of competition. *Subtract 9 points from your current score.*

Seething Time Bomb: Ted "Unabomber" Kaczynski parlayed the genius-about-to-blow thing into a decade-long career as America's most elusive architect of terror, and became a poster boy for this image type. Warning: You may have to live in Montana to pull this one off. Second warning: Death penalty now mandatory for all crimes. *Subtract 7 points from your current score.*

Bland Golfer: Are you the kind of person who wants to prepare for death by acting dead while technically alive? Are you Presbyterian? German-American? Do you drive a Caprice Classic? Part your hair on the side? Would you ever wear a Ralph Lauren shirt? The Bland Golfer image might be

for you! Warning: Your offspring will be seething time bombs. *Subtract 2 points from your current score.*

Energetic Go-Getter: If you want people to wonder how much coffee you drink, this is the persona for you. As an Energetic Go-Getter, you'll drag your ass out of bed at five in the morning, run 10 miles, and still be at your desk by 8:00 A.M., ready to trade

futures on the commodoties exchange. You'll be married, have two paramours on the side, and cheat on your taxes so well you'll still pass the audit. You'll zip home on the parkway, meet your eight kids at the door after school, and play with them all before falling asleep during the six o'clock news. Warning: Death will ensue on or before age thirty-seven. *Subtract 8 points from your current score.*

Failed Dreamer: "I wrote the Great American Novel," the Failed Dreamer asserts, "but I got so pissed off at how stupid everyone is that I burned it up. So there." And people will actually believe him. The Failed Dreamer never has to attempt anything because nothing is really worth doing and we all just die in the end anyway, don't we? *Subtract 4 points from your current score.*

Now tally up your score. If the resulting number is positive, you've chosen a childhood appropriate to the image you'd like to project. If you come up with a negative number, try again. If you can't get a positive score after three attempts, consider physician-assisted suicide.

You may ask yourself whether a stupid test like this can possibly lay your psychological demons to rest. If so, stop wondering—it can't. The point is, *perception is reality.* The image you project will determine how you're treated, how much you're paid, whom you get to have sex with, and who will hang out with you. Once you're starring in your own sitcom about giant ants and you're dating Brad Pitt or Winona Ryder, who cares about that time your mom drove nails through your hands to make you understand the pain that Christ felt two thousand years ago?

As Eldridge Cleaver might have said if he had been a pop psychologist, choose your childhood—and your buttocks will follow.

4. DIVORCE FOR FUN AND PROFIT

"The Chinese character for crisis is the same as the one for opportunity."
—*Dumb philosophical cliché*

So your family as you knew it has just gone the way of the Edsel and the Commodore 64 computer. Half of your aunts and uncles have vanished from your life, the two people that you are biologically encoded to rely upon for food and CD money aren't talking anymore, and, if you're under eighteen, the college of your choice has just been replaced by the college you can afford.

Big deal—you're just a typical American.

When I hit the first grade in 1968, I was the only kid I knew whose parents were splitsville. By 1976, when I began junior high school, I knew about a half-dozen children of divorce. By the time I graduated from Fairmont West High School in 1981, about one in four Americans my age were products of "broken homes." Now the national average is at least half. After a 1990 peak, when two out of three new marriages were doomed, the marital success rate has leveled out at roughly 50 percent. Sure, divorce is still a traumatizing event, but it's become a typical one, a rite of passage like learning to swim and going to the prom.

Everyone knows the downside of divorce. The lemons-to-lemonade question is: How can you turn the wholesale destruction of your family—the worst thing that can possibly happen to a human being—into an advantage?

First of all, forget all that bright-eyed optimism crap, as well as the psychiatric twaddle that kids are sturdy enough to survive their parents' divorce. Divorce sucks more than anyone who hasn't been through it can imagine. But it's also a fact of life—if not your life, the life of a close friend—so you might as well make the most of it. Moreover, success is the best revenge, especially if you suspect that you weren't valuable enough to make your parents stay together for the sake of the kids. Your parents are each looking out for numero uno—and so should you.

So, toward the end of mitigating a few of the ickier aspects of the Big D, here are some of the advantages of having divorced parents:

You get to choose which parent you prefer. Unless one or both parents aren't in any way interested in custody, they'll be vying for your tax deduction by any means necessary.

Legally, a family court judge will determine custody, but if you're ten or older, you'll have a big say as to which home you end up living in—especially if you're articulate and presentable. If you're under ten, you can always return to court yourself when you're older. Think of the advantages: Is your mom too broke from a lousy alimony settlement to buy you a car for your Sweet Sixteen? Is your dad an uptight prig who'd object to your having sex in your room? Your role in the custody battle is to choose the lesser of two evils and play them off against each other—it's just like voting! (Beware of the growing "joint custody" arrangement, a kid-under-the-shell scheme that involves shuffling you back and forth every few days. It may seem tempting not to have to choose one parent over the other, but this setup leaves you completely without negotiating leverage. Complaining about feeling torn between the two homes as well as worrying aloud about inconsistent schools and neighbors are good tactics to derail a joint-custody arrangement.)

Play Spy vs. Spy. Your parents will probably refuse to employ traditional methods of communication, like the phone or e-mail, with each other. Instead, they'll rely on you to transmit their demands and petty remarks back and forth during court-ordered visits. Understandably, this is a role that many children of divorce despise. But it also offers numerous advantages: When the noncustodial parent says, "Tell your father you could use some new clothes the next time you see him," this request can be slightly altered to a more suitable one, like "Hey, Dad—Mom's threatening to take you to court for more money, but I'm working hard to talk her out of it. Any chance of you buying me a new DVD player today?"

The sympathy vote is yours. Once you start dating, you'll find that half of your prospects have intact families. These are people who imagine that, as a child of a broken home, you've suffered enormously. Since this will be at least partly true, it should be an easy matter for you to regale them with sad tales of pathetic Christmases or Kwanzaas or whatever, as well as whole weeks without food. Bat your mournful eyes at them. Typical remark: "Seeing all this happiness really depresses me." I have often parlayed the sympathy of the dual-parented into tasty meals, business relationships, and even sexual favors. You owe it to yourself to get on the growing victimization bandwagon!

You get a new family. It may be hard to believe now, but at some point, despite your own shattered family history, you'll probably find yourself contemplating tying the knot yourself. Children of divorce have much bet-

ter relationships with their in-laws than do "normal" people, and you may find that you actually like them better than the human beings to whom you're biologically related. No cheap family loyalty for you; you get to choose between up to four parents—more, if your spouse is divorced as well!

You'll save on presents. It's normal for the noncustodial parent to eventually lose interest in you. This can take minutes or days, but when he (it's usually the "he") stops returning your calls, you'll know that this has occurred. He will remarry, possibly to some inbred, inane, and physically unappealing crone with eight kids she got stuck with when her third husband ran off with the dishwasher repairwoman. Sure, you'll hear from the guy now and then, but almost no one is able to maintain a close relationship with the noncustodial parent. After all, this is the person who didn't care enough about you to pay a lawyer to bribe a judge to issue him custody. Words of protest to the contrary, you know the real deal. You don't owe the noncustodial parent anything more than a birthday card, and then not necessarily on an annual basis. Presents, phone calls, and concern for the absentee parent's medical problems are superfluous and should be avoided. Don't feel guilty about it—just use the extra cash you would otherwise have had to buy yourself a little consumerist joy. Or, if you're truly shrewd, buy your custodial parent extra goodies—and watch your clout increase!

You can channel your anger for fun and profit. Countless musicians, authors, and alternative cartoonists have parlayed their shattered families into lucrative careers. Such celebrities as Kurt Cobain and River Phoenix have owed their success and subsequent deaths—which made them cultural icons— to their fucked-up family lives. Dealing with the fact that the people who made love to make you can't talk a minute without yelling may drive you to drink, but try to avoid alco-

holism and excessive use of narcotics as much as possible. You'll be far happier, and society will be much better off, if you commit your rage to poignant lyrics and heavy black drawings of guys getting their heads blown off. Plus it beats working in some depressing office without a decent ventilation system.

You'll enjoy guilt-free parent disposal. Whether you keep one or both parents after the breakup, you'll be so alienated from the whole concept of family that you'll have no guilt about sending either parent to hell if they give you a hard time. The benefits of this advantage cannot be overstated. You'll actually feel sorry for your friends as they struggle to deal with their married parents' unreasonable, abusive, and annoying behavior—without any escape.

Charting the correct course through a divorce will provide you with excellent training for exploiting the rest of life's postmodern crises—so, if your parents still get along, now may be the time to start thinking about breaking up their marriage!

5. COLLEGE IS FOR SUCKERS

"Oh, my God—It's Senior Year! All you care about is your career!"
—*Dead Kennedys, "Life Sentence," 1982*

n Stephen King's novella *The Long Walk,* the biggest event in postapocalyptic America is an annual race-walk featuring a hundred boys. To ensure a lively pace, flatbed trucks carrying soldiers shadow them along the side of the road. Whenever a boy's speed falls below three miles an hour, the soldiers bark out a warning. After the third warning, shots ring out, and the laggard drops to the asphalt. The contestants hike down I-95 until they're either blown away or fall over dead from exhaustion.

The last survivor, the guy who outlives his ninety-nine competitors, receives The Prize from the nation's mysterious, charismatic dictator. The Prize is anything the winner desires. The Prize is all anyone ever talks about. After the crowds go home, however, the winner is taken out and quietly executed. You don't need an actual prize to motivate the participants, after all—merely the idea of a reward will do the job.

In preapocalyptic America, parents force their kids to run an eighteen-year-long marathon for a similarly futile remnant of the American Dream called The Promise. Graduate from the right college, The Promise goes, and you'll learn all you need to know to land a good job, meet the right mate, and have a great life. The catch is that you have to survive countless filters—grades, tests, demographics, occasional bad luck—to get into a good school. For the lucky few, being admitted is merely a prelude to the ultimate challenge: finding the cash to pay those insanely high tuition bills. For most, the only answer is to take out huge student loans, setting up yet another financial gauntlet to survive long after graduation. In no time at all, The Promise says, you'll pay back the loans, earn more money than the losers who didn't make it, and leave your kids an obscenely huge inheritance.

THE PROMISE DEBUNKED

College makes you more marketable, especially during difficult times. Although there are subtle advantages to being a college graduate when you're looking for work, the difference is slight compared to the cost of tuition and fees.

Highly competitive admissions processes select the best and the brightest. Given the way our society selects who will go to college, there is little evidence of this. Having worked in the admissions office at a highly competitive university, I can assure you that the process is arbitrary as hell. Often the best and the brightest don't stand a chance.

Without a college degree, you will shrivel up and die like a desiccated bug. Actually, you might be better off both financially and professionally if you go straight into the workforce after high school.

Although the best way to ensure a high-paying job is to major in something "practical," a liberal-arts degree is better than none at all. Nope. There's no financial advantage to going to college as a liberal-arts major.

College is a worthwhile learning experience, vital to shaping the leaders of tomorrow. Nah. College students mainly learn how to get drunk, fuck, and pass out.

I understand The Promise well. My entire life was devoted to the single goal of gaining admittance to and financing attendance at a prestigious Eastern university—ideally an Ivy League school. In eighth grade, I planned out all fifty-six of my high school classes through senior year, and I stuck to my plan. I worked three jobs to save money for school, but kept money in cash so the financial aid office wouldn't take it into consideration. I joined countless extracurricular activities because I thought they'd help me get into a good school (I can still feel the polyester outfit I wore in marching band while playing the clarinet part to "Don't Cry Out Loud [Just Keep It Inside]"). Like most teens, I wanted to go to parties and have girlfriends, but I worked on extra-credit assignments instead. I couldn't let anything stand in the way of escaping my Ohio suburb.

Because I'd done well in math and science in high school, my mom insisted that I pursue an engineering degree at Columbia University. (Parents often confuse academic ability for interest.) "Look at your dad," she said. "He makes good money. Do something practical, something that will guarantee you a job when you graduate." I thought that she was right.

But courses like Nuclear Engineering E3001 and Partial Differential Analysis G4305 didn't hold my interest for long. I slept through almost every course, either in bed or in class. Three years later, I'd racked up an impressive string of Ds and Fs, particularly in physics. Since physics was my major, this was bad. When my dean called me to tell me that I'd been expelled, he told me that he couldn't decide whether it was for academic or disciplinary reasons. I had twenty-four hours to vacate my dorm.

I eventually went back to college, and graduated in 1991. But since then, the Promise has evaporated. Measured by traditional indicators like the Dow Jones average and the unemployment rate, the American economy has boomed, but not so that the

average employee could notice. Not only are corporations not hiring, but they've laid off 43 million people, some more than once, since 1979. From 1990 to 1994, the top 5 percent of wage earners saw their paychecks rise 17 percent. The rest of us lost ground. Under such dismal circumstances, college has become a major detriment to achieving the American Dream.

Most Americans go to college in order to land on the first rung of the comfy, safe corporate ladder. Now that those corporate jobs are either low-paying or nonexistent, we should ask ourselves:

WHY GO TO COLLEGE?

Nazi physician Josef Mengele decided who lived and who died at Auschwitz. Mengele always took time out of his busy schedule to greet every shipment of prisoners, even

when he had a cold. The SS doctor "selected" the fate of every man, woman, and child who arrived by cattle car with a brusque wave of his right hand: To the right meant a slow death from starvation and overwork; to the left led straight to the crematoria.

In America, first- and second-grade teachers armed with IQ exams disguised as "aptitude tests" mark kids as either college or 7-Eleven bound within the first few months of school. From that point forward, the fate of American children is virtually predetermined. Nonetheless, college-tracked students are expected to spend the next twelve years preparing for the college application process. Even for the fortunate who have been selected, a minor slipup can lead to developing an intimate knowledge of deep-frying.

So you've gotten into the school of your

dreams? Don't ease up now! The same vicious atmosphere of competition prevails here—you'll need the right grades to get the right college-recruitment offer from the right company, or even to make it to graduation. Given up on the job market? You'll still need at least a 3.5 GPA to get into a good graduate school! The treadmill never ceases.

Until the day your heart stops beating, people will ask you where you went to college. Your answer to that cocktail-party question will often determine what people think of you, what jobs you'll be considered for, whether or not you'll be promoted, whether your in-laws will approve of you. Your glowing personality, savvy wit, and stunning achievements can overcome an education deficit . . . if you're lucky. You won't even be safe from the cult of college when you die; your alma mater will rate a prominent mention in your obituary.

IS IT WORTH IT?

Once you cut through all the hype, the financial and emotional sacrifices Americans make to send their kids to college just don't yield the payoff that many of them are looking for: financial security.

Politicians from Federal Reserve Chairman Alan Greenspan on the hard right to former Labor Secretary Robert Reich on the muddled left blame our current economic problems—downsizing, increasing income disparity, the trade deficit—on the need for more education. Bipartisan support for a concept often implies its truth, but in this case it's more of a conspiracy. Why are people of such divergent political backgrounds lying to us?

Experts say that there's no correlation between education—even a technical education—and increased income. American workers haven't suddenly been rendered obsolete by technological improvements. In fact, the United States already has the most highly educated workforce in the world—25 percent of our workers are college graduates. Logically, we should be kicking serious ass in the global economy, but we're falling way behind. Blame our economic problems on the decline of unions, greedy CEOs, excessively free trade, a regressive tax structure, the lack of an electric fence along the Rio Grande, whatever you want. But it's not caused by insufficient education.

CERTIFICATION, NOT EDUCATION

We take for granted that a four- to eight-year stint at a college or university is required to mold an American into a well-rounded, educated *homo modernis*. In ancient Greece, the relationship between students and teachers was personal, customized, and intense. Today's colleges and universities are anything but.

At Columbia, I met countless student-idiots: kids on football scholarships who passed classes without attending them, children of wealthy alums, pupils who cheated

on almost every exam they took. One time, when I was working as a math TA, I tutored a woman in the "help room." We kept breaking down a calculus question until I found the actual problem—she didn't know her multiplication tables.

Although America's universities are churning out a steady stream of brain-dead simpletons, our society relies almost exclusively on college credentials as the central determining factor of social status and employment opportunity. "A college degree is a signal to employers that you can do what people tell you to do for four years," Patrick Barkey, Ball State University's director of business resources, says.

COLLEGE TUITION OR MUTUAL FUNDS? NAME THE BETTER INVESTMENT IN TWENTY WORDS OR LESS

Our society devotes enormous resources to the quest for a college diploma. In fact, the

United States is the only industrialized country that relies on individuals to foot most of the bill for higher education.

At any given time, roughly 8 million full-time students each pay an average of $19,000 per year in tuition and board fees—a total of $152 billion. This is equal to more than half of the federal budget deficit. During the eighties, health-care prices rose 110 percent, an increase that sparked the current health-care imbroglio. Meanwhile, the cost of

attending college rose 109 percent for public schools and 146 percent for private schools, but no one's panicking. They're too busy writing out checks.

As with most things that Americans buy but can't afford, they borrow the money. They took out $19 billion in guaranteed student loans in 1995, and that number increased with new Clinton administration loan programs.

"The shift in emphasis of federal student

aid from grants to loans threatens to create a generation of debtors," said American Council on Education president Robert H. Atwell. And, it's happened—in the late eighties, 23 percent of student loan borrowers defaulted.

And the program is only getting bigger. In 1992, Congress removed the ceiling from a program that allows parents to borrow up to the total cost of four years' tuition and created a new, unsubsidized loan option that permits undergraduates to borrow up to $10,000 annually—without considering financial need. Rates are higher, too—up to 13 or 14 percent from the old 9 percent.

IT'S MORE THAN JUST COED DORMS: THE FINANCIAL ADVANTAGES OF COLLEGE

If, like most Americans, you consider a college education to be a certification process—a means to a high-paying job—then there are reasons to take out big loans to pay that bill (tuition, books, housing, food, and other expenses typically total $25,000 a year for private four-year colleges and $15,000 for public institutions):

- You're less likely to be unemployed.
- You'll make more money.
- You'll make more money over time.

There's no doubt that our society rewards those brave souls who have met Milton, Thucydides, and Einstein on the academic fields of battle. For one thing, your old college pals can hook you up with good jobs later in life. But you liberal-arts majors won't share in the economic spoils. The degree differential pays off almost exclusively to those who go the professional route—particularly in engineering and

medicine. One year after graduation, humanities majors earn less than workers of the same age without any college education. Even biology majors won't see a dime of payoff for passing those brutal organic chemistry exams. The only winners are the 20 percent of students who majored in health care, engineering, math, physics, and computer science.

The 80 percent of college students who are liberal-arts majors are getting screwed—or screwing themselves. And if you're majoring in something like art history . . .

It gets worse. In the early 90s unemployment for liberal-arts majors exceeded the national jobless rate of 6.2 percent. Those irritating health-care majors had a low 1.0 percent jobless rate, engineers 3.2 percent, and computer scientists 5.1 percent. On the other hand, 6.7 percent of psychology majors spent their afternoons watching *Ricki Lake*. History majors were the kings of the

dole at 8.2 percent. (Hey, Mom! Guess what I finally majored in?)

COLLEGE AND EDUCATION: ARE THEY RELATED?

In some ways, I benefited from Columbia's liberal-arts approach to higher education. Although I hated spending time and money on required classes, I would never have learned about the architectural significance of the Seagram Building, the poet John Donne, or Soviet innovations in astronomy if they hadn't been shoved down my throat.

On the other hand, most of school is a waste of time. For full-time students, classes take up fifteen hours a week. If they're diligent, they may study and work on assignments another fifteen hours. The rest is downtime. I fondly recall numerous naps, soap operas on TV, marathon sex sessions, and observing my friends' drug habits.

Not that sex and TV and sleeping are bad or anything, but should we spend four years of our lives—and a hundred grand—fucking and sleeping?

Arguably, most classes are worthless too. Many are taught by inept graduate students or professors with no interest in teaching. Grades are capricious. When I returned to Columbia I discovered that the following statement vastly improved my chances of landing an A: "I'm an A student. Could you tell me what I need to do in your class to get an A?" I went from a 2.4 to a 3.8 GPA in my second incarnation as a college student. Coincidence? I don't think so.

Worst of all, most students learn to regurgitate information rather than think for themselves. They take notes as their professors blather on and on, but rarely question them out of fear of getting low grades. They read books outside class, then they come in to be told what they mean.

Ultimately, they've been programmed for employment.

In an ideal world, education would be customized to the needs and desires of every student. In reality, college students work through codified curricula that fit a school's lowest common denominator. This rote regurgitation that passes for thought is excellent training for working as a corporate drone, but it's not an education.

IVY LEAGUE OR BUSH LEAGUE?
THE PRESTIGE DIFFERENTIAL

Assuming that you've decided to pursue an undergraduate degree, where should you go?

Differences in the quality of education are subtle. Professors at Ohio's Wright State University are just as likely to have earned their doctorates at Yale as are professors at Yale itself, though whether that makes them

better teachers is debatable. At state universities, instructors tend to be less accessible due to large class sizes, especially for your first two years. However, the big-name schools' small class sizes tend to get canceled out by the pressure on professors to do research and publish. By your junior year, it's essentially the same deal either way, whether you attend City College or Cornell University.

To be sure, attending a "prestigious" school has its advantages. Many of your classmates will be rich, influential pillars of the community someday. Conceivably, *these people could help you later on.* Among my classmates at Columbia were a Moroccan princess, Martha Stewart's daughter, and Dan Rather Jr. I tutored the princess in calculus at exorbitant rates, attended Dan's well-funded parties, and spied Martha's winsome tax deduction in the cafeteria now and then. It may not have done much for my socioeconomic status, but learning how the white power elite is trained came in handy for lampooning them in my cartoons. Before I went East, I'd always thought "crew" was a hairstyle. Making it to Harvard won't grant you admittance to the American aristocracy, but it will put you on a first-name basis with it.

On the other hand, opting for a lower-cost state school will save you about $40,000, which makes up for the reduced snob appeal. If you're willing to seek it out, you can get just as good an education at Eastern Kentucky State University as anywhere else.

Although compromise is often the best solution to consumer dilemmas, attending a second-tier, not-quite-Ivy institution like NYU or Amherst offers the worst of both worlds. You'll wallow in rush weeks, pep rallies, and date rapes and still shell out

$25,000 a year for a degree that won't even raise an eyebrow at the HR offices of the snootier firms. Most lists of "good education buys," such as *US News & World Report*'s annual "Best Colleges" issue, snub these second-tier schools.

GET SMART WITHOUT GETTING EDUCATED

Why play along? If you really need a cumbersome bureaucracy to teach you what they want to teach you because you're too unimaginative to learn on your own, and the idea of a four-year vacation from life appeals to you, start rounding up recommendation letters and application fees. If you need college certification to pursue your professional goals, go for it.

Otherwise, bear in mind that The Promise, whatever its merits during the fifties and sixties, is a quaint anachronism dating to an unwritten social contract that

has long since been revoked. Inexplicably, our politicians and pundits are trying to turn the U.S. into France, where Sorbonne graduates drive taxis and collect unemployment. Trained for an elite without openings, these stillborn technocrats can't find it within themselves to start their own businesses, write software, sell stuff on the street, or whatever it takes to survive in a world without guarantees. They bought into the notion that a college degree is everything and they still can't believe they were lied to. They expected to coast through life after graduation, so they focused all their energies on the day when they'd walk down a long aisle to collect a diploma. They lived for that moment, and once it passed, their lives were over.

They do have one big advantage over Americans, though: They may be rote-fed social propaganda, but they don't have to pay for the privilege.

INSIDE THE BELLY OF THE BEAST: THE MYSTERIES OF AN IVY LEAGUE ADMISSIONS OFFICE UNVEILED!

I've seen the Rubik's Cube of college education from every possible point of view—applicant, discipline problem, and honors student—but my perspective wouldn't be complete without the other side of the process. I worked for two and a half years in an undergraduate admissions office at Columbia University. I handled hundreds of admissions and financial aid applications, following every step of the application process from a person's first request to be mailed a catalog to his first request to drop a course.

What I saw made me wonder why employers are so ready to rely on a college degree as an indication of ability. Admissions and financial aid in particular were subject to a nasty witches' brew of nepotism and politically correct maneuvering. The typical

CAN YOU ANSWER THESE SIMPLE QUESTIONS?

These are the kinds of things we need to know to compete in the international marketplace. We can't tolerate half-wits if we're going to take on the Indonesians. Can't hack it? Do the right thing: kill yourself. Or we'll do it for you.

AMERICA: IT'S OPEN SEASON ON MORONS.

middle-class applicant stood no chance whatsoever of receiving a scholarship. Having a parent who earns $25,000 a year—which isn't enough to live on much less save for college—was enough to disqualify a student. They could, however, get as many student loans as they wanted—at ever-increasing interest rates.

One year, the school's highest need-based scholarship went to a woman whose annual income was $36,000 in interest earnings from investments. She got it because she licked the dean's ass, which I suppose was good training for life in the workplace. The dean justified it because the student was a woman. Meanwhile, we turned away poor kids from the Bronx because they couldn't pay the tuition.

Admissions was just as much of a farce as financial aid. First, as at most universities, admissions committees are a myth. There aren't any. Applications are divvied among the admissions officers, who make 99 percent of acceptance and rejection decisions individually. Most students' fates are based on their GPAs and test scores, in that order. In marginal cases (at Columbia, a GPA of 2.5 to 3.0), extracurricular activities come into play, but it's rare. Affirmative action policies are formalized when admissions officers multiply test scores by factors based on race.

Most of the educational bureaucrats who make the Big Decision are poorly paid, third-rate losers who are too untalented to do anything else. Because admissions officers receive low pay (around $28,000 to $34,000 at Columbia) and few chances for raises or promotions, the job attracts unambitious older slackers. They like the light workload and outstanding benefits of working inside ivy-covered walls—free use of the university gym, a generous retirement plan, and no dress code, not to mention access to attractive young students.

Atypically, my division was blessed by two admissions officers who were perceptive, amusing geniuses. The third, however, was an insufferable, moronic hardass. Aware of her predilection for arbitrarily rejecting people, we *Untermenschen* gave her all the admissions applications of students we didn't like. If we had it in for someone, we could "misplace" his file until it was too late for a decision to be made for that term. Alternatively, we greased the skids for our friends. We'd go to the dean and give her the old "His grades don't reflect his abilities" speech, and supply our pal with essay tips (for instance, don't begin your essay with: "On Tuesday, September 17, 1980, a baby girl was born. Her name was Caitlyn."). This often made a big difference.

Even the lowliest clerk (I was an office assistant)

affects admissions decisions. If someone gave me a lot of shit over the phone, I'd mark him a "20" (do not admit/pain-in-the-ass) or "19" (insane). His application wouldn't make it past my file drawer. A lot of applicants are transfer students with several transcripts from various colleges, often of varying quality. If I liked someone, I could pull her unfavorable transcript until after she'd gotten admitted, then drop it back into the file so she'd still get her transfer credits.

If you didn't get into the school of your choice, don't worry about it. The decision process is so screwed up that admissions and rejections don't say anything useful about the people getting admitted and rejected.

American colleges turn out hundreds of thousands of total idiots every year, and millions of geniuses are working the night shift at Arco. Truly educated people learn on their own—at school, at home, on the bus. Everyone else is just going through the motions. It's too bad your next potential employer doesn't know this.

6. YOUR LAWYER, YOURSELF

"You're scum. Your client is scum."

—*Precinct commander to attorney, in* Robocop, *1987*

hen I was still young enough to have heroes, I worked my way through such 1970s icons as Johnny Bench, Joe Strummer, and Barbara Jordan. The Reds player, Clash singer, and Watergate congressperson were each worthy of that special place in my heart, but, in turn, each was deposed. While other great heroes came and went, my mom's divorce lawyer remains in my mental pantheon.

My mom and I would surely have starved to death after my dad walked out on us if our attorney hadn't fought him in court. He not only squeezed cash out of my pathologically cheap dad, he repeatedly dragged him back to court over the next two decades to make him fulfill his obligations under the divorce decree one line at a time.

So I don't share the American view of lawyers as parasitic, cynical scuzbags. As far as I can see, lawyers are the best friends an average American can have. I *love* lawyers. They've saved my butt countless times.

When my college roommate (whose name isn't really Mike) and I left Manhattan for a road trip to Cape Cod, I knew he was an incorrigible pothead. What I didn't know was that Mike had brought along an extra batch of "supplies" from the South Bronx. After flicking on the headlights a few seconds too late, we got pulled over and busted by a small-town cop in central Massachusetts on suspicion of driving with out-of-state plates.

After a night in jail, my whiny—yet effective—letter convinced the best lawyer in town to take on our case pro bono.

"Here we have two young men, college men, who made a mistake," this massive Italian-American pleaded. "Everyone's entitled to one mistake, right?" Sounded reasonable to me. More important, it sounded reasonable to the judge, who coincidentally happened to be our attorney's former partner.

We were both acquitted of Possession of Narcotics Class D and he convinced the judge to permanently expunge the arrest from our police records. The judge's trust in me has since turned out to be well placed; my life outside the law has been limited to occasional speeding and driving alone in the carpool lane. Mike can't say the same, having intimately experienced the New York City corrections system on several occasions, but a 50 percent recidivism rate isn't bad.

A few months later, I got expelled from Columbia on suspicion of not attending class. As if catching the academic boot firmly in the buttocks of my résumé wasn't sufficiently injurious, my ex-alma mater billed me $3,300 for a senior dorm room I never got to occupy because I'd been thrown out of school. I went through two years of earthly purgatory attempting to get the university to tear up the bill, but neither the bursar, the collection agency, nor the civil court would see reason.

Finally, I called the local bar association for a referral. They sent me to an attorney whose practice is devoted to representing students in lawsuits against Columbia. (In 1957 he had been expelled from Columbia Law School for publishing an exposé of the school administrators in the law review.) Two days later, for the modest fee of $750, he had Columbia off my back.

As someone who draws political cartoons for a living, my job is to offend as many rich and powerful people as possible. One of the numerous occupational hazards cartoonists face is that politicians and corporate executives get angry at you. Sometimes they merely send cease-and-desist letters, but just as often they file lawsuits for libel, slander, defamation, or whatever. These suits are nearly always as frivolous as they are well funded. On the rare occasions when they're right, you can always issue a public retraction.

The last time I ran into legal trouble, I was targeted by a company famous for its Christian fundamentalist CEO because I called him a "right-wing Christian nutcase." Shaking off his dogs required four law firm partners on both coasts.

In recent years, juries have practiced a lot of income redistribution. When a Bronx jury awarded one of subway vigilante Bernhard Goetz's four victims, all of whom were violent criminals, $43 million, many right-wing corporate types brayed that it was a classic example of the need for tort reform.

Businesses and government often cite a civil court verdict awarding tens of millions of dollars to a woman scalded by McDonald's coffee as an example of jurisprudence gone berserk, but ask yourself: How would you feel if a company's stupidity caused your grandmother to get heat blisters on her genitals?

In the McDonald's case, the jury heard that the company had ignored hundreds of complaints about its dangerously hot coffee, and I remember it myself—it really was too damned hot. It took a multimillion-dollar judgment to wake the company up.

In another case that aroused a lot of media coverage, the New York Metropolitan Transit Authority lost millions in a court ruling in favor of the family of a blind man who mistook the space between subway cars for the car doors. He fell to the tracks and got run over by the train. Newspaper editorials called the case absurd, but the fact remains that subways are now equipped with accordion-style

LAWYERS TO WATCH OUT FOR
THE WARNING SIGNS

Lawyers. I love them, you love them, we all love them together. But when you're facing ten-to-life for passing those three Ks of Turkish hash to the wrong undercover cop or trying to sleaze out of that pricey paternity suit, you can't afford to take any chances with a merely "average" lawyer. Memorize this list and do *not* hire any lawyer who:

- Advertises on matchbooks and daytime TV
- Has an 800 number that spells out "DAMAGES"
- Requires money up front "to cover me in case something happens"
- Charges under $100 an hour
- Has signed photo of Al Sharpton on office wall
- Has signed photo of O.J. Simpson on office wall
- Dates Marcia Clark
- Doesn't have a key for the hall rest room "because of misunderstanding with the landlord"
- Uses Kinko's
- Wears bow tie, knit tie, bolo tie, or string tie
- Has phone book listings under different first and last names
- Claims that he cares
- Keeps framed diplomas from three Kuwaiti high schools in office
- Has office in cruddy building in cruddy neighborhood
- Has snazzy office in upscale neighborhood
- Says "These things take time"
- Says "I don't want to take your money"
- Has Burt Bacharach tunes piped into phone while you're on hold
- Has picket line outside office
  (Exception: If pickets are cops, hire immediately.)

devices between cars—an improvement that benefits all riders, not just the blind.

Municipalities grouse over runaway litigation, but they do nothing to prevent it. New York City admits that it pays out more in settlements and jury awards to the owners of cars damaged by potholes than it spends on street repairs, yet it continues to neglect road maintenance. If the congressional promoters of tort reform have their way, the scalded granny, the minced blind guy, and the owner of the Accord with a broken axle would have no recourse. In corporate terminology, what happened to them would simply be tough shit—and if the company goons in Congress have their way, we'll soon have no ability to sue to recover damages for these atrocities. As it is, Americans are increasingly forced to waive their right to sue in order to receive basic services from corporations.

Police salaries are paid by us taxpayers, but "our" cops prowl the streets of our cities like troops occupying an invaded country. Social constraints have evaporated. The government is supposed to look out for us, but it's too dependent on money from profit-mad corporations with bottomless pits of cash at their disposal. We can't count on business to do what's best for anyone other than its top executives. Given the absence of anyone else to protect us from incompetence, idiocy, and violence, lawyers are our last line of defense. Admittedly, many lawyers are opportunistic, exploitative hacks, but they're all we have left.

That's why I recommend that everybody keep a lawyer on retainer at all times. In fact, many people, such as those in more than one line of business, need several attorneys. You never know when some moron with a grudge or merely having a bad day will sue you, or when your rights will get stomped on by some person or institution. Fortunately, the old Wild West days, when every dispute could be settled by emptying a gun into someone's skull, are over. It's far more civilized, and better for the country, if you drag those who did you wrong through the court system. Don't worry about cluttering up the courts; if dockets get too crowded, the government should hire more judges and build more courtrooms to match all the new jails. Suing is your sacred right as an American. Always remember that those who would limit civil court judgments are trying to protect rich lawbreakers from ordinary people like you.

I just hope no one sues me over this.

7. SLACK OFF FOR A BETTER AMERICA

"Work is for suckers."
—*Bart Simpson*

David Bowie sold out in 1980. Bill Clinton sold out from the start. Kurt Cobain started to sell out but blew his brains out instead, ensuring himself a high place in the pantheon of the principled. It's important to note that what constitutes selling out for some people—working for a big corporation, changing one's image or work to conform to an accepted norm, being nice to people you hate—is mere pragmatism to others.

What these differing views of workplace integrity all have in common is that they emphasize the *style* of work. Work itself is never called into question; we take for granted that everyone has to earn a living, except for the few people, like children and Kato Kaelin, who survive by living off other people's work.

When Thomas Moore, Chairman Mao, and Jerry Rubin suggested that work might not always be necessary, they were not talking about their own times, but rather some period in the far-off future when technological progress and better social organization would allow everyone to sit around watching TV, building model airplanes, or whatever else their little hearts desired. They thought that such a time was a long way off, but it's here now. We're just too corrupted by the work cult to see it.

CASE STUDY:
THE SAN FRANCISCO EXPERIMENT

In August 1994, I got a job as a financial analyst at a San Francisco consulting firm. The company's clients are banks looking to increase their profitability, either by increasing their fees without their customers noticing or by merging with other banks. It's a very nineties company, not only because it deals in information, but also because of its corporate culture. Before I was hired, my boss, Emma, told me that I could set my own hours, take vacations whenever I felt they were justified, and dress however I wanted. In short, the only thing that mattered, she said, was that my work—mainly cranking out spreadsheets and charts—got done. In return for my services, I would be paid $32,000 a year. As a cartoonist whose big break wasn't yet on the horizon, I

was happy to work in a windowless, airless office and considered myself fortunate to have a job with flex-time where nobody cared what color tie I wore.

But once I started, Emma told me that while I could set my own hours, I would have to be in by 8:30 A.M. and leave no earlier than 6:00 P.M. Vacations were also greatly encouraged—in theory. But when you actually asked for a specific day off, you got that look. (If you've ever held a job, you know the look—it's that same narrow-eyed stare your

mom used to give you when you were up to no good.)

So, despite the company's rhetoric and quarterly New Age–style retreats where a licensed therapist "analyzed the company's dysfunctionality," what I had in reality was a generic full-time job.

At first I had a difficult time learning where everything was and how the computer system worked. But after a few months, I was surprised to find that I could finish all of my work in about two hours a day. This came in handy, because I could use the remaining six hours engaged in far more satisfying activities, such as calling newspaper editors, sending out faxes, talking to my friends on the phone, and jerking off in the rest room. I learned to schedule my official work at times when the nosy office manager was around or when my boss wasn't on the phone. The only complaints about my performance arose

really smart, efficient spreadsheets would have made the day go by quicker and the company's output look better. But that was never in the cards—corporate hierarchical systems always demand the same old stuff day after day after day.

My experience was, I have learned, typical of many jobs—style outweighs substance. For instance, it soon became evident

when my strategy failed and I got caught printing out personal correspondence on the printer. No one ever complained about my actual output, which was always praised as well written, concise, and thoughtful.

I never understood why my employers paid me so much money to sit around and do nothing. Although I apparently did what was expected of me (including taking advantage of their stupidity), it was a bummer not to be given any challenging assignments. Sure, they were just spreadsheets, but creating

that my professed low-key New Age employers had a distinct dress code for men—baggy tan trousers and yuppie button-down shirts. Any deviation from this uniform would bring about subtle reproaches, such as: "All you ever wear is black jeans and a T-shirt."

To be at work by 8:30, I had to get up at 7:00. I'd never be home until 7:30, and the commute between San Francisco and Berkeley on BART's stifling trains was grueling. I'd go to sleep at midnight, which meant that I spent more than two-thirds of my waking hours going to work, being at work, or coming back from work. And for what? To produce a few hours of mediocre spreadsheets to go into reports sold by a mediocre company for the basest of reasons—to enable the mass exploitation of my fellow consumers.

I have always suffered from an excessive awareness of my mortality. I feel every second, every minute, of my life slipping by, bringing

pers. But I had to sneak around, always terrified that my boss would catch me. I would have been far more productive—and true to myself—doing the same personal stuff at home. Even my personal phone calls, of the whispering, paranoid variety, were low quality, and thus prevented me from achieving everything I could for my personal benefit. And ripping off my boss was getting to be as

me closer to my death, gasping and wheezing on a sidewalk at some point in the future. There is no greater sin than wasting your time. You'll never, ever get it back. What could be a worse sellout than squandering your life force five days a week, fifty weeks a year?

But that's what I did at the consulting firm, as I have at every other place I've worked. Admittedly, I had roughly six hours a day to build databases to help me market my cartoons, learn how to use layout programs, and write articles for magazines and newspa-

bad for my soul as the job itself. But there were always those bills to pay.

Eventually, I got so desperate for something to do that I requested additional work. It was mainly to alleviate my boredom, but also to try to make myself more useful, and therefore fire-proof. Afterward, a few more assignments hit my desk, but my workload still amounted to roughly two hours per day. As for the time I spent doing company work, that was almost completely worthless as well. I would lift charts and graphs out of pub-

lished sources, compose them into the computer format we used, and insert them into client presentations. A good scanner would have worked just as well. And that's not even getting into the moral implications of my job: contributing to mergers that caused massive layoffs and bank-fee increases that hurt consumers and added to the nickel-and-diming of America.

In short, my job—and it was a pretty decent job, as jobs go—was a giant waste of time.

I noticed that my superiors—Baby Boomer former middle managers who'd been laid off from various banks in the late eighties—also worked roughly two hours a day. Unlike me, they didn't have a side career to develop, so they used their six-plus hours of "face" time in such pursuits as organizing their children's soccer teams and dealing with illnesses, gossiping with one another about their surly underlings who wore black jeans and T-shirts, and planning exotic trips to foreign lands.

OVERVIEW:
WORK EXPERIMENT UNSUCCESSFUL

Some employers are starting to catch on to the fact that not a hell of a lot of work occurs at "work." Many big corporations are laying off a worker every twenty seconds. The official unemployment rate hovers around 5 percent. That number doesn't include "discouraged workers," people who don't even bother looking for work anymore. It doesn't include part-time workers who would rather be working full-time or people who are "underemployed"—Harvard MBAs working as secretaries, for example. Full-time workers have become part-timers; professionals have become manual laborers. The fastest-growing jobs in this "information-based economy" are janitor, nurse, and food service worker.

Much of what passes for politics these days concerns placing blame and proposing solutions for a shortage of decent jobs that dates to the 1970s. Lefties blame greedy, short-sighted corporate executives whose tireless search for cheap labor causes them to shrink their payrolls—thus constricting the pool of disposable consumer income. Conservatives cite government's unwillingness to train students to become "competitive" in the new global economy.

The left believes corporations have an obligation to employ people they don't require. Although it's true that downsizing often hits those who do the actual work for the benefit of management pigs who don't, no one should have to employ workers rendered obsolete by technology. The right and its corporate allies want a "more educated workforce" even though they can't challenge the workers they already

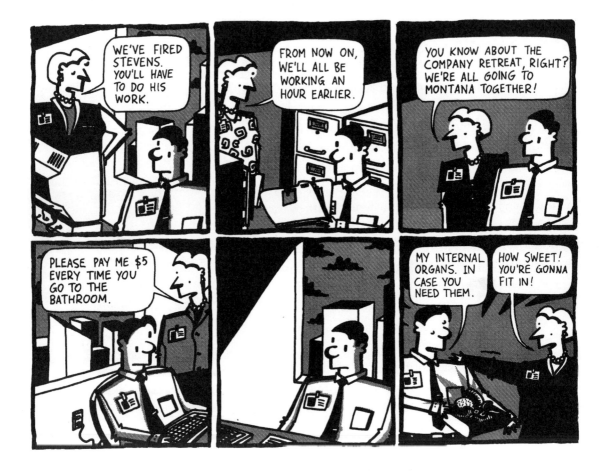

have. Both sides simply refuse to adjust to a world with fewer jobs.

Jobs are disappearing without significantly reducing productive capacity. The technological advances predicted by nineteenth-century utopian philosophers have finally occurred. The trend of increasing unemployment and underemployment ensures that we're all going to have a lot more idle time, whether we like it or not. Under such conditions, working for a corporation isn't what makes you a sellout; *it's whether you work at all.* The real dilemma is how to learn not to work when we don't have to.

Work is going out of style. The truth is that the only reason most people want a job is because they have bills to pay. Certainly society doesn't need everyone to work; the only interest government has in reducing unemployment is to keep people off the streets. Some workers mark time, collecting paychecks and hoping no one will notice that they really don't do anything. Others toil at double jobs, filling in for downsized former colleagues at the same pay. It doesn't make any sense to argue about what kind of job makes you a sellout when jobs are entirely about getting paid and not at all about the kind of work being done. In a world where work itself compromises your soul, who's the worse sellout, a senior vice president or a clerk?

CONCERN:
WORKER ALIENATION

Selling out is really about alienation from your labor. In 1957, the philosopher Fritz Pappenheim neatly encapsulated the Marxist definition of alienation as the state of mind that occurs when people are separated from the fruits of their labors.

My analyst job was a classic case of worker alienation. I got to see only a small part of the final product—my three pages of charts in a seventy-page report. I wasn't advised what the presentation was for, and I never met the client. When I was able to piece together the overall purpose of the project I was working on, I'd usually discover that it was an effort to reduce the expenses of some banking corporation in a state I'd never visited. Moreover, it was impossible to derive any kind of satisfaction from work that took two hours a day to complete but required eight hours of face time to ensure my continued employment.

I found every single second I spent working for those people impossibly annoying, just as I have resented every other job I have ever held. I felt robbed of the few hours I spent actually working. More and more, younger Americans are feeling bitter about wage slavery, even if the wages and conditions of servitude are fairly decent. Back in the Eisenhower years, workers were willing to tolerate the mind-numbing nature of working for somebody else as they marked time toward a cozy retirement with a company pension plan and a Winnebago. Now that corporate and employee loyalty are dead, however, work must be its own reward to get people out of bed in the morning. No wonder the slacker ethos has finally come of age.

Your employer takes away time and energy you might have invested in yourself. For example, I could have drawn a cartoon or two for every day I spent at work—but because our economy is structured around wage slavery instead of self-employment, I would have starved. Working for a company is like renting—you earn money to pay your bills, but have developed nothing you can use to further your own future. Working for yourself, on the other hand, is like buying equity in a house.

The only person at the firm's San Francisco office who really worked full, nonstop days, evenings, and weekends was Wendy, its chairman and founder. And why not? She owned the most stock and got her picture in the paper and her name at the top of the letter-

WORKING FOR THE MAN VS. SELF-EMPLOYMENT

CONSIDERATION	WAGE SLAVERY	SELF-EMPLOYMENT
Hours	40, plus whatever they tell you	40, plus or minus whatever you tell yourself
Wages	Fixed at rate of inflation, at best	Possible range from destitution to limitless wealth
Benefits	Low-grade medical and dental plan, 401(k)	None
Job Security	Can be fired at any time	Economy can go to hell
Future Prospects	You'll have to change jobs anytime you want a real raise	Anything's possible

head. She was the only one there working for herself. Everyone else was just a wage slave—even the yuppies with six-figure incomes.

CONCLUSION:
GET PAID MORE—WORK LESS!

The obvious answer is for us to work *less*, not more.

When I was seven, in 1970, my father bought me a box of Cracker Jacks. The prize was a little booklet about how life would be in 1980. In 1980, it predicted, people would be scooting around in hovercrafts rather than cars and working ten-hour weeks. What happened? In 1949, the workweek averaged around thirty-eight hours, labor unions talked of bargaining for the thirty-hour week,

and the military-industrial boom of the 1950s and 1960s was still in the future. Now we're working forty-eight-hour weeks, labor unions are all but gone, and we're still not seeing the difference in our paychecks. Somehow the trend of reducing the workweek that dominated labor-management negotiations in the first half in the century was reversed; workers started taking their raises in the form of salaries instead of time off.

As Juliet Schor, author of *The Overworked American*, says, society could choose to exploit the postwar productivity gain in any of several ways:

• We could all have double salaries.
• We could be working twenty-hour weeks.
• We could work six months a year.

SELF-EMPLOYMENT: THE REVENGE

Instead, some of us are working multiple jobs with insanely long hours for low wages, while others can't find work at all.

The money generated by that hidden boom in productivity didn't disappear. The vast majority of it went to create an unprecedented upper strata of wealthy Americans.

The United States now sports the greatest chasm between rich and poor in the industrialized world—1 percent of its population owns 40 percent of its wealth. We live under a corporocracy that pays $40 million to CEOs and $8 an hour to file clerks—in the same company! Unless you are one of the fraction of 1 percent of Americans who belong to this new elite, your hard work is benefiting some rich white guy—not you.

The more you work, the more you contribute to this increasing disparity of wealth and its resulting social instability. At least in

the old days, when you sold out you got paid for it. Now you don't even receive a bigger paycheck—someone else does.

OVERVIEW:
WORK IS FOR SUCKERS

As big business continues to lay off people, eliminate jobs by attrition, and downgrade existing positions, the message has become clear: They don't need us.

Why can't we accept that our services are simply no longer required and move on? We demand that companies hire people they no longer want or need, that the government subsidize employment through jobs programs, and that other countries somehow stop competing with us to cut us some fiscal slack. Why can't we take a hint? It's over. Computers are replacing us at the office. Robots have our jobs at the plant. The company picnic, the gold watch, hanging out by the watercooler, and time clocks are all part of an anachronistic lexicon that people of the twenty-first century will struggle to remember while playing trivia games. They don't need us anymore, but there is hope:

You can't sell out if there isn't any market for your services.

QUERY:
IS WORK GOOD FOR YOU?

Cursed by our hard-ass Pilgrim founders—remember, these people were so uptight that they couldn't get along with the *English*—we have been programmed to believe that work for work's sake is an intrinsic human virtue. We've been taught that all human progress to date was the direct result of innovation, sweat equity, and hard work. Relaxation was merely an unpleasant precursor to what really mattered: work. What were we thinking?

ANDY HERDED SHEEP, TRADED STOCK, COOKED, PERFORMED SURGERY, BUILT REFRIGERATORS, PLAYED GUITAR, FRIED BURGERS, STRIP-MINED, FARMED, DESIGNED ADS, DROVE TAXIS AND DEALT CARDS AT A CASINO. ANDY DID EVERYTHING.

FOR A LONG TIME, EVERYONE WAS HAPPY. THE IDLE RICH HAD VIRTUALLY ELIMINATED LABOR COSTS. THE IDLE POOR WERE ALL ON THE DOLE. ANDY WAS TOO BUSY TO BE MISERABLE.

CAN YOU FIX MY WATCH? AFTER I DESIGN THIS BRIDGE IN ZAIRE.

FINALLY: AN 8% TIP? THAT'S IT—I QUIT! WAIT! YOU CAN'T QUIT!

Rather than view it as a social ill, Americans should embrace widespread deemployment from traditional jobs. Isn't this the fruit of our long struggle to improve the way we live by developing new technology? Most people aren't needed to work anymore, so why should we call the unemployed lazy? And from the perspective of the young, salaries and benefits are low, the work is boring, and advancement is nonexistent.

While allegedly working at the San Francisco consulting firm, I decided that there is almost no financial inducement to hold a job. The truth is, technology has put millions of Americans out of work, yet the economy has never been better. On the micro level, those who do the least—executives—earn the most. In America, the less you work, the better you do. Inefficiency is driving the greatest economic expansion since the fifties; working hard is bad not only for our souls but also for our entire way of life. That's why every American should rebel against the employment fetish with the following techniques:

Just say no to work. An unbelievable number of Americans hold jobs without needing them to pay the rent: kids whose parents want them "to learn the value of a dollar" (hint: It's one hundred cents), people whose spouses make enough to support both of them, those who've inherited enough to work little or not at all, people from wealthy families. These individuals, not to mention their drug-addled children, would all be much happier, and more productive, if they stopped working. They would also be improving the lives of those still stuck in the workplace by reducing the available labor pool, thus improving salaries and working conditions.

Slack off for a better America. Every employee owes it to himself and to his nation to do the bare minimum of work required to avoid getting fired. Nap in the rest room, pull the fire alarm, disconnect customers, jam the photocopier, break the fax machine, pour coffee into the computer—anything to reduce the efficiency and output of your place of employment. Reduced efficiency increases the need for labor, ensuring better treatment for the proletariat!

Depress your boss. At every opportunity remind your boss about the futility of the company mission, the worthlessness of his job, and the sheer pointlessness of work. During meetings, gaze dreamily out the window and wonder aloud whether it would be a good day to fly a kite or take the kids to the park, and analyze how totally stupid the task at hand is compared to the fact that global warming will eventually make the whole country look like Venice. This will be an

arduous duty, but absolutely necessary to eradicate work from everyday life.

Get fired. There's nothing like the special feeling of freedom one gets from getting the ax. Sure, you're worried about money, but you're also free. No more asshole boss, no more stupid schedule. You can go to the beach or the park! You can catch a baseball game! You can sit in a café reading Pappenheim's *Alienation of Modern Man!*

You'll discover that you're hardly alone. Every day, Monday to Friday, eight to five, millions of people are walking around the streets, free as the wind. Why not join the armies of people who've given up on the rat race? Go to your boss and say, "Fuck off, you ugly, pea-brained, rat turd." (Later, when you file for unemployment, vehemently deny that you were fired for cause; otherwise, you won't get benefits.)

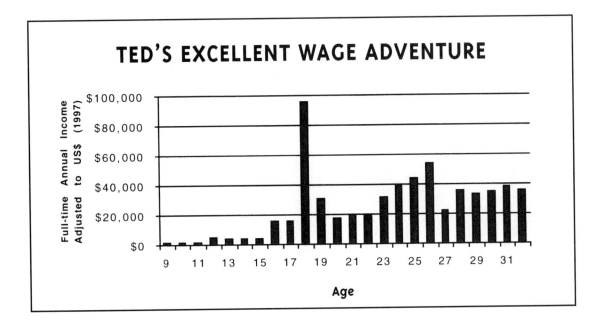

TED'S EXCELLENT WAGE ADVENTURE

ADDITIONAL QUERY: WHAT CHOICE?

Sooner or later, the United States will have to acknowledge that work as we know it—the forty-plus-hour-a-week variety—has become obsolete. Economic and technological trends ensure that the ranks of the unemployed and underemployed will continue to grow for the foreseeable future. If we continue to ignore this demographic shift, social disintegration is inevitable.

Regardless of how one defines selling one's soul, what could be more corrupting than to work long hours at a meaningless job? Not only do you sell yourself to a machine that doesn't care about you, but you contribute to the decline of society as you do it.

But waiting for the government to wise up isn't necessary. It's up to individuals to make the decision not to work. In my case, I got fired from the consulting firm due to my bad attitude. Apparently I hadn't kept my personal phone calls, faxes, and side projects sufficiently secret (not that my employers knew the half of it). My instinctive response to getting canned, as someone who has worked his entire life, was to start looking for another stupid job.

But I didn't. My wife and I decided that rather than start looking for another day job, I should concentrate on cartooning. I had won a journalism award earlier that spring, after which I'd picked up some new newspapers and received some favorable press. To make up some of the $500 a week of post-tax income

I used to collect from my day job, I sought out freelance illustration work. I started working on a new comic book and a new weekly column. And I filed for unemployment. California unemployment paid me $230 a week —they don't buy "bad attitude" as an acceptable reason for firing someone. Suddenly, I didn't miss my salary anymore.

No more day job for me. I just wish I'd thought of it myself.

THE DIGNITY OF WORK:
One Guy's Quest for Upward Mobility

Below are listed all of the jobs I have held since I first began working for money. I have not included freelance or odd jobs. As the ambitious son of an immigrant, I have struggled to climb the ladder of middle-class success since I was nine. I am now thirty-four. As a result of my efforts, I co-own a car.

AGE/DATES	JOB DESCRIPTION	EMPLOYER	SALARY	BENEFITS	REASON LEFT
9–14 1972–77	Mowed lawns and trimmed shrubs	Huber Rental Homes Kettering, Ohio	$7 per lawn	Sometimes people don't notice when you don't rake the trimmings	I'm allergic to cut grass; cheap people made me wait until lions were running through the grass to cut it
13 1978–79	Blackboard cleaner and locker cleaner	Barnes Junior High School Kettering, Ohio	$3 per hour	Found money and office supplies in other kids' lockers	Pedophile janitor tried to feel me up in a locked classroom
12–15 1975–78	Newspaper deliverer	Times Publications Kettering, Ohio	$20 per week	Drunken subscribers sometimes give you big bills without noticing	Not enough money; gray bull terrier on route that liked to bite and bite and bite
15–17 1978–80	Newspaper deliverer	*Dayton Journal-Herald* Dayton, Ohio	$25 per week	None whatsoever	Had to get up at 4:30 A.M. every day; got frostbitten during blizzard
16 1979–80	Bag boy	Freedom Foods Kettering, Ohio	$2.65 per hour	Stole groceries and returnable bottles; cute female cashiers	Got fired in the wake of the mother of all food fights with another bag boy, involving several cases of Ragu, Clorox, and raspberry preserves
17 1980–81	Dishwasher	Friendly's Restaurants Kettering, Ohio	$2.90 per hour	Got to wear durable polyester uniform and eat discounted food	Scalding water, no tips, smelled like day-old burger lard all the time, closed at 4:00 A.M. on school nights
16–18 1979–81	Editorial cartoonist	Times Publications Kettering, Ohio	$30 for 2 cartoons per week	Kids at school thought I was cool; made fun of local politicians	To go to college in New York

AGE/DATES	JOB DESCRIPTION	EMPLOYER	SALARY	BENEFITS	REASON LEFT
17 1980	Playground supervisor	Dept. of Parks & Recreation Kettering, Ohio	$3.20 per hour	Got to play games and raise hell with kids	Got caught, along with kids, dropping water balloons and dead fish off the freeway overpass
18–19 1981–83	Teacher's assistant	Columbia University Math Dept. New York City	$20 per hour	Great money; occupied professor's office when he was out; access to women students	Job eliminated by Reagan-era budget cuts
19 1982	Traffic engineer	City Dept. of Transportation Kettering, Ohio	$6 per hour	Unsupervised work in souped-up city car that used to be a cop cruiser; spent whole days at the pool	Fired for general immature behavior including, but not limited to, chasing friends' cars with the siren and lights of my city car on
20 1983	Work-study assistant	Columbia University Libraries New York City	$4.25 per hour	Stole office supplies; drank beer at lunch; napped all afternoon in the office supply room, which inexplicably contained a cot	Quit while bosses were meeting to fire me after someone saw me on a beach-bound subway train on a day I called in sick
20–21 1983–84	Math and history tutor	Columbia University Tutoring and Translating Agency New York City	$25 per hour	Great money; billed parents for hours of watching TV with students	Had to commute to obscure sections of the Bronx; students complained to me when they got bad grades
21 1984	Math and history tutor	Trinity School Prep-for-Prep Program New York City	$12.50 per hour	OK money; met psychotic, brilliant high school senior who shot out windows of adjacent housing project while chatting with me on the phone	Affirmative action victim; middle-aged white male boss told me the kids needed a Latino or black (preferably female) role model
21–22 1984–85	Computer programmer	Merit Audio/Visual New York City	$5 per hour	Unsupervised work; watched soap operas when boss was out	Fired for theft of bicycle (actually stolen by another employee); later sold "my" software to rival company
21–24 1984–87	Taxi driver	Hudson Street Garage New York City	$150 per night	Good money; independence; reckless driving with someone else's car; occasionally picked up women from Queens coming home dateless after a night of clubbing	Fired after totaling cab and two parked cars on West End Avenue with damage of $22,000; would have quit anyway after being mugged three times (one gun, two knives)

AGE/DATES	JOB DESCRIPTION	EMPLOYER	SALARY	BENEFITS	REASON LEFT
22 1985	Trader trainee	Bear Stearns & Co., Inc. New York City	$10,000 per year	Same exact work as guys earning 100 times as much; all-male locker-room atmosphere	Same exact work as guys earning 100 times as much; all-male locker-room atmosphere
22–26 1985–89	Taxi driver	23rd Street Car Service New York City	$110 per night	Good money; independence; reckless driving with someone else's car	Quit after receiving taxi ticket and being mugged, both in three hours
23 1986	Administrative assistant	Bankers Trust Company Jersey City, New Jersey	$17,500 per year	Better money; company cafeteria had incredible view of lower Manhattan	Fired for being out sick the entire third week I was there and refusing to work overtime
23 1986	Computer programmer	American Institute of Physics New York City	$7.50 per hour	No supervision; mellow bosses; free long-distance phone calls	Laid off after completing six-month project in three months
23 1986	Trust administrator	Bank of New York New York City	$22,000 per year	Money	Quit after one day when boss used jargon like "learning curve" and "team player"
23–27 1986–90	Assistant loan officer	Industrial Bank of Japan New York City	$36,000 per year	Good money; boss cool beyond belief; free sushi and French food; exposure to nuts and bolts of capitalism	Had to wear Brooks Brothers suits to work in building suffering from sick-building syndrome; eventually would have been laid off due to lending freeze; quit to go back to school
24 1987	Manager of English school for Japanese executives	Metropolitan Language, Inc. New York City	$35,000 per year	Chance to start own business	Business killed by investor's wife, who wanted more of her husband's money for herself
25 1988	Telemarketer	Ed Blank Co. New York City	$6 per hour	Learned how to lie through my teeth on the phone; still comes in handy	Depressing work; depressing coworkers; shitty pay; general loss of dignity and sanity
25–26 1988–89	Music critic	New York Observer New York City	$1 per word	Huge money; tearsheets; free concerts and records	Newspaper editor stopped returning my calls (Hey! I'm still here!)
26–27 1989–90	Music critic	National Alliance New York City	Kept review LPs	Tearsheets; free concerts and records	Cultlike organization wanted my soul as well as my records; no money

AGE/DATES	JOB DESCRIPTION	EMPLOYER	SALARY	BENEFITS	REASON LEFT
26–27 1991	Taxi driver	18th Street Car Service New York City	$80 per night	Money	Quit after a week due to poor money and lack of air-conditioning in June
28 1991	Office manager at hot-sheets motel	The Regency Islander Motel Vallejo, California	$100 per night	Weird, *Repo Man*-like ambience; daily dialogue with welfare moms, ex-cons, gang members, Vietnam vets	Tired of patrons complaining of low-quality X-rated movies ("Who are you, fucking Siskel and Ebert?"); moved back to New York City
28–33 1991–96	Syndicated cartoonist	Chronicle Features San Francisco	$900 per month	Dream job; what I'd always wanted to do; exposure to millions of people; chance to meet other cartoonists	Moved to bigger syndicate
29 1992	Math tutor	East Harlem Counseling Services New York City	$20 per hour	Good money; close to home	Quit after losing temper with two kids who broke a classroom window and then being praised for it by boss
29–31 1992–94	Office assistant, grade 6	Columbia University Admissions New York City	$22,000 per year	Laid-back; virtually no supervision; mindless work	Quit to move to California and escape moronic student applicants ("Hi. I'm calling about, uh, school. You have classes, right?")
31 1994	Illustrator	*Rolling Stone* New York City	$750 per piece	Great money; exposure; chance to meet Hunter S. Thompson	Editor stopped returning my phone calls; never met Hunter S. Thompson
31 1994	Office manager	Dancing Tree Paper & Printing Berkeley, California	$28,000 per year	Desperate for a job, any job	Psycho boss charged 25¢ "stupidity charge" for every clerical mistake I made
31–32 1994–95	Financial analyst	"XYZ" Corp. San Francisco	$32,000 per year	OK money; didn't have to wear a suit to work	Got fired for bad attitude, not being a "team player"
33– 1996–	Syndicated cartoonist & columnist	Universal Press Syndicate Kansas City	$3,100 per month	See 1991-96, Chronicle Features	Still doing it

Business as Usual

WASHINGTON (API)—The recent trend of renaming public spaces in order to raise revenues came into its own today as the White House announced that the presidential mansion will from now on be referred to as the Exxon House.

Press secretary Leon Panetta said that the international petroleum corporation paid $175 million for the name change, which will go to service interest on the national debt.

Vice President and President-Elect-Apparent Al Gore applauded the move, saying: "When we talk about reinventing government, this is what we're talking about. When we sell off our national heritage, we're selling something that never cost us a cent!"

Panetta also declared that other presidential icons would soon be put up for sale. "Everything from presidential tiepins to the Oval Office itself will be offered either for sale or for long-term lease," he said. "You wouldn't believe how many paintings we have of presidents nobody even remembers, like Fillmore and Agnew.... It's all first come, first served."

Please see editorial, "Smart Move for Clinton," page 312.

8. MAKING THE MOST OF YOUR DEAD-END JOB

"What, you afraid to get your hands dirty, college boy?"
—*My boss, ordering me to dispose of poisoned wharf rats, 1982*

They just don't make jobs like they used to. Even for the well educated, "entry level" rarely leads to what used to be called the "career track." These days, workers are damned lucky to have a job at all—or at least that's what we're told all the time. Getting trained for more responsibility? A big raise? Rapid-fire promotions? Maybe in those cheesy eighties flicks starring Michael J. Fox, but not in today's corporation-dominated world. It takes more than hard work and loyalty to get you to the top—nowadays you have to be born there.

Whether you toil in the mailroom or the executive suite, chances are you're earning a low salary (especially compared to what the big shots down the hall are getting) with little prospect of anything more than token increases that barely keep up with inflation—plus there's a good chance you'll get canned the next time the Dow takes a southward turn.

If you earn more than $30,000, you're kicking relatively serious fiscal ass—but you probably have to work late every night and come in on weekends to get that paycheck. Net result: Your hourly rate (because you're on a flat salary!) isn't any more than the lesser-ranked support staff you'd like to look down on.

Whatever you do, don't fall for the trap of believing that because you wear a suit and tie, or a suit and black pumps, you're management. You're management if you don't do any real work, if you spend your days getting soused with clients while planning dates with your mistress. You're management if you earn six or seven or eight figures, plus bonus, with a company car and free stock in the firm. Wearing a white shirt, or being white and male, doesn't make you management. If you're reading this book, you probably aren't management.

ARE YOU A TEAM PLAYER?

The other big pitfall to avoid is feeling as if you're "part of the team." When you collect a paycheck from The Man, you're an employee. A subordinate. An inferior.

More likely, like the 90-plus percent of workers who told *The Wall Street Journal* that they were smarter than their bosses, you're a wonderful, talented, attractive, hardworking person. But it's important—absolutely vital!—that you understand your position in the pecking order, which depends on what your boss thinks of you. If your desk is as

beautiful as his, and your office looks as well appointed, and the title on your business card is no less impressive, then this advice isn't for you. But the vast majority of Americans work for someone else, not for a "team."

To your employers you're less than nothing, worth less than the computers and other equipment they really need to make money. Corporations take care of the equipment because they need it. Computers won't work if they're abused or exposed to excessive heat. Human beings, however, can be squeezed for everything they're worth and are easily disposed of. And why not? People under the heel of hierarchy must grin serenely while they stifle their screams of frustration and anger.

MAXIMIZE YOUR OUTPUT, DUDE

Fundamentally, this is the free-market system we live under, one in which the relationship between worker and employer is always intrinsically exploitative, combative, and adversarial. In recent years, we've absorbed endless corporate propaganda about how unions are unnecessary in an age of unprecedented labor-management cooperation. The unions promote something called the Team Concept, under which workers are supposed to feel as though they have real decision-making power because they choose the color of the break-room paint. Unions have evaporated to the point that they represent almost no one, and many workers have been convinced that their fates are tied to the financial health of their employers.

In fact, working hard is no guarantee that you'll be around to share in the good times after you've sacrificed long hours for the company. What's good for the company has nothing to do with what's good for you. You have to look out for yourself; giving even a passing thought to what's good for your boss's business makes about as much sense as a mouse commiserating with the horrendous

day-to-day problems faced by the cat. Just as the boss's duty is to get you to work as much as possible for as little pay as possible, your duty should be to work as little as possible for as much pay as possible.

The problem is, how can you do this without a union to represent you? These days, you have to pay yourself. That means extracting the salary you really deserve and the time off you really need by, as Malcolm X once said about loftier matters, any means necessary.

Bear in mind, however, that not every employer deserves to be ripped off. At its most basic level, work is the exchange of labor for wages, but when people spend most of their lives at work, it becomes much more than that. Employers treat their charges like children. If bosses have become surrogate parents, they ought to act like responsible moms and dads—by taking care of their workers' medical and dental expenses, paying for their education, and giving them plenty of time to go outside and play. Managers who aren't willing to fulfill both sides of the bargain are exploiters, pure and simple, and fully merit the shaft.

I have held a variety of low-paying clerical jobs over the years, all of which passed the exploitation test. My bosses all expected the world while giving out diddly, and I in turn never failed to exploit each one to my best advantage.

JOB ENHANCEMENT FOR FUN AND PROFIT

If you can become a mail führer, by all means do it.

At one job, I maneuvered myself into the exclusive control of the office's postage meter machine.

I was able to parlay a $20,000-a-year job into a $45,000-a-year one through abuse of the mailing privilege. It's no exaggeration to say that without my own personal franking privilege (hey, if it's good enough for Tom Foley . . .), I would not have been able to fully develop my career as a cartoonist. There was no way I could have afforded to send out hundreds of dollars a month in mailings without my so-called job—and these mailings gave me the edge when I was fighting for editors' attention.

REACH OUT AND TOUCH THE BOSS

Find some way to steal long-distance service from your employer. In big firms, the conference rooms offer both privacy and open long-distance lines for clients to use. At small ones, if you have to bill your long-distance calls to a client, do it! Just use some colleague's phone, preferably someone you don't like, while they're out of the office. Another classic trick is making calls from the fax machine; those lines are almost never encoded.

SICK OF BEING SICK

You'd be amazed how many people never use their sick days. If you leave the company, you'll lose those days off, and they are yours to take! Think about it—in Europe, they get six weeks' paid vacation every year, not two measly ones like here.

Consider it your holy duty to yourself as a human being, as well as to your fellow workers, to become unwell as often as possible and elevate America closer to the European model.

MULTITASKING IS YOUR FRIEND

Computers are great for slackers, since it's easy to work on the Great American Novel at your desk without anyone knowing. Smart people arrange their desks so that the boss can't easily see what they're doing as he walks by. Just to be safe, you should always have a legitimate work project up and running so you can switch to it on your screen at a second's notice. I have written countless letters, proposals, and essays, including a few chap-

ters of this book, while on company time. Multitasking—or producing work for pay while on an unrelated clock—vastly increases your net salary and ensures that your time at work wasn't completely wasted on pointless drivel for someone else.

PROPERTY IS THEFT, AND VICE VERSA

At retail jobs, you must shoplift. After all, your boss fully expects it; he's even built a 10 percent theft rate into his financials! My friends have recounted an infinite number of sordid tales of every possible scam from smuggling books and CDs to emptying out the place through the back door in the middle of the night with the help of an illicitly copied key. Whatever you do, don't get snagged, and don't work somewhere that sells stuff that you don't like (not everyone should work at the health-food store, for example) or that can't be easily resold. Ideal job: pharmaceutical assistant!

SO IT'S YOUR FIRST INTERVIEW
Here's What to Look For

You've lied on your résumé, your roommate has posed as Bill Gates to recommend you, and the suckers have invited you to their office. How will you know whether this gig is worth taking? Here are some points to consider during your visit:

Are there holes in the wall?
Fist-shaped holes in the office wall indicate that your predecessor was downsized, outsourced, or just plain canned. Never take a job that became available as the result of a firing; the odds are you'll be next.

How about e-mail?
If your potential employer uses internal e-mail, beware: The Supreme Court has ruled that they can read everything you send. Unless you want your boss to know every time you log on to a kiddie-porn chat room, forget it.

Does the boss travel?
Is the boss The Thing That Won't Leave, or does she have more frequent-flyer miles than Robert Vesco? An absent boss is a good boss.

Is there a human resources department?
A sure sign of bloated bureaucracy. Organizations that employ HR personnel are inefficient and clueless. Think of the fun you'll have!

How old are your colleagues?
Is the place crawling with Volvo-drivin', white-wine-swillin', baby-sitter-bonin', Summer-of-Love-nostalgin' fortysomethings who actually expect you to work for The Man? If so, this probably isn't the place for you. Look for the relaxed, ass-dragging young'uns who make every workday a holiday.

How old are the computers?
A company that recently updated its Wang system is not long for this world. More important, your personal text files won't translate well to your next office's system.

Is there a vacation or sick day policy?
Nothing is worse than being told to take sick days or vacation days whenever you want or need them. This nonpolicy policy makes it next to impossible to take a day off without looking like a slacker, which, if you're smart, you are. Ask for a defined policy, and take advantage of every last day that's owed you.

Analyze phone responses.
In accordance with standard procedure, your interviewer's phone will ring at least once during your interview. Observe him/her carefully. Is he/she polite? Calm? Does he/she scream "Don't ever call here again, you parasite?"

Check for jargon.
The most pernicious threat to a happy workplace is the use of corporate jargon. Does your interviewer ask you which "team" you'd like to "join"? Does he use the term "learning curve"? Does he throw around acronyms that no one understands? No matter what, do not take this job—you'll be better off on welfare.

Although you should be able to make up for your employer's exploitation by robbing him blind, I have found that entry-level clerical jobs offer by far the best opportunities for the creative criminal mind. It's hard for your supervisor to keep track of what you're doing, you have access to lots of cool office equipment like copy machines, and somehow employers don't seem to expect to get ripped off by their pseudo-yuppie staffers. Forget crappy gigs like bartending and waiting tables—the only people who benefit from your sucking in secondhand smoke all night are the lame friends you ply with free drinks and discounted food.

If you're normal, stealing will probably cause you to feel occasional pangs of guilt. Clearly, this is dumb. Sure, you've been taught that stealing is wrong and that laziness is a negative personality trait. And theoretically, that's true. But stealing from your employer isn't stealing per se; it's merely a partial restitution: The boss is stealing your time and energy and sapping your life's blood to make himself some extra cash. As for the "laziness," getting away clean is a real chal-

lenge! And if maintaining a tiny shred of human dignity for your sad self reflects sloth, so be it. Who wants to end up like the millions of middle managers downsized in the last twenty years—pathetic, used-up wrecks who sacrificed family and fun to increase profits in which they didn't even get to share?

Every job offers its own unique opportunities, and you must be sharp to take advantage of them. But 100 percent exploitation is your goal, since it's also the goal of your employer to exploit you totally and absolutely. Don't ever think otherwise—every time you come home from work having put in a long day for your boss without making a personal phone call or working on a personal project, without having stolen time or merchandise, you have screwed yourself. And if there's anything worse than exploiting a fellow human being, it's allowing yourself to be exploited without even indulging yourself in the joy of passive-aggressiveness.

Keep your dignity. Make Them think you're a loyal drone, but work mainly for yourself—it's the only way to make the best of your bad situation.

TED'S EMPLOYEE BILL OF RIGHTS

I. In light of the invention of such devices as the telephone, fax, and Internet, business travel is obsolete. If, nonetheless, you must travel to strange and boring cities, you have the right to be left free and unmolested by your coworkers in the evenings. Morning meetings shall be punishable by hard labor in Alabama or, if Alabama is unavailable at the time, by hard labor in another undesirable southern state.

2. Any employer who requests that an employee come to work on weekends or holidays shall be shot. No stone shall mark his grave; none shall mourn his passing.

3. Working before or after standard work hours shall be strictly prohibited. Police shall search offices for signs of after-hours labor and raze any buildings where such work is found to be occurring.

4. Anyone who asks an employee to bring work home shall be publicly garroted.

5. A full one-hour lunch shall be guaranteed by law. Violations of this provision shall be punished by the destruction of the offending boss's home and the donation of his pets to local animal shelters.

6. Obtaining coffee and/or food shall be each person's responsibility. No person shall request another to perform such tasks on his or her behalf. Offenders shall be doused with hot coffee.

7. Any increase in responsibilities shall be matched by an increase in salary commensurate to the additional time and/or effort required.

8. Employers caught setting the office clock back shall be publicly flogged.

9. No more than two sets of revisions shall be permitted to any report, document, or project.

10. No employee may be fired, canned, laid off, downsized, or otherwise shitbagged by any company reporting a profit during the previous fiscal year. Violators will be nationalized.

9. AMERICA ON $100 A DAY

"If you have a big enough inheritance, it doesn't matter how ugly,
or ill-mannered, or stupid, or lazy you are."
—*My economics professor, 1990*

You've traded in your stolen street signs and cinder-block bookshelves for real pressboard furniture from Ikea. Your typical evening used to involve Rudy Ray Moore videos and a case of generic beer; now you watch those same movies over bottles of house red stolen from your night job as a waiter. When you got out of college back in '91, you were entering names and addresses into a computer, but those days are over: Now you *train* the guy who enters names and addresses into the computer.

These are all certain signs that you've finally entered adulthood. It took a little longer for you members of the underemployed and overeducated generation that grew up in the shadow of the Baby Boomers to make your collective mark, but there can no longer be any doubt that you've finally come of age. And an important part of adulthood in a postindustrial economy is to prepare for your financial future.

taxes. That's why I'm forming my own army, sanitation service, and post office."

Azalea's independence will serve her well as she plans for retirement. But Xers will need more than their trademark cynicism to survive in a twenty-first century blessed with rising floodwaters, airborne pollutants, and mutant stillborns. We've asked some of the nation's leading financial planners what measures today's Xer needs

Unlike their demographic forebears, today's young adults know that they won't be able to count on Social Security or Medicare to save them from selling their organs to the wealthy after they lose their last job at age sixty-five. As Azalea O'Dowd, a twenty-seven-year-old assistant manager at a Wendy's restaurant on the I-270 bypass outside Marietta, Georgia, says, "The government doesn't owe us anything in return for our paying 40 percent of our income in

to take to ensure a sound fiscal future. Here's what they had to say:

INVEST PRUDENTLY, YET AGGRESSIVELY

"The average young adult typically has $12 in savings," notes Dartanian Poisson Jr., an analyst at Future, Inc., the Austin-based consulting firm. "I would take $5.50 out of the bank, where it's earning maybe 2 or 3 percent in interest, and split it up 40 percent into an aggressive growth fund, 30 percent into a standard S&P 500 index fund, and invest the remainder in precious metals, like platinum, to hedge against the inevitable sociopolitical collapse of the year 2028." Poisson would invest the remaining $6.50 in a film, either "a thriller like *Air Force One,* or maybe one of those Dutch movies about people who sleep with people they're not supposed to."

Caitlyn Aziz, senior vice president of the

RETIREMENT PLANS:
NOT JUST FOR THE DYING

"Retirement is more than just the twelve years between the end of work and the end of life," says Taniqua Aziz, who recently left her sister's company of Niechwiadowicz, Gallapokalis and Aziz to form her own firm specializing in long-term planning, The Taniqua Aziz Experience, Inc. "If I were a young adult today, which I am, I would take

Niechwiadowicz, Gallapokalis and Aziz investing group, agrees with Poisson, but notes that movies now cost $9 in big cities like New York and Los Angeles.

In any case, those savings, supplemented by depositing 1 percent of every paycheck to those funds for the next thirty years, should yield about $14 at retirement after broker fees, taxes, and cyclical recessions. "It may not seem like much, and it isn't," says Poisson, "but consider the alternative."

advantage of my firm's 401(k) or traditional defined-compensation program.

"Of course, self-employed people like me don't have access to these programs," Aziz says. "You have to stay at the same large company the rest of your life in order to collect them, which means that there aren't any real retirement plans anywhere in the United States."

But there's still reason to be optimistic: Since most Gen Xers are paid low salaries,

they simply won't be able to afford retirement anyway.

TRADITIONAL SAVINGS

Many financial experts worry that today's young adults, who aren't accustomed to setting aside their money into regular savings accounts, won't have enough spare cash in the event of an emergency. "My grandson says he can't save because he only earns $7 an hour—but lack of money is no excuse not to have savings," asserts Eli Mojave, the

seventy-two-year-old Wall Street wiz now serving an eighteen-month sentence for securities fraud at the Squaw Valley Correctional Facility.

Poisson, the consultant, has clients who actually save more than they earn, and Taniqua Aziz sets aside $20,000 of her $30,000 annual salary. How does she do it? "Don't pay your taxes," Aziz advised us by coded cell phone from an undisclosed location. "I also sell synthetic narcotics to Gulf War vets. It's a victimless business, as everyone knows."

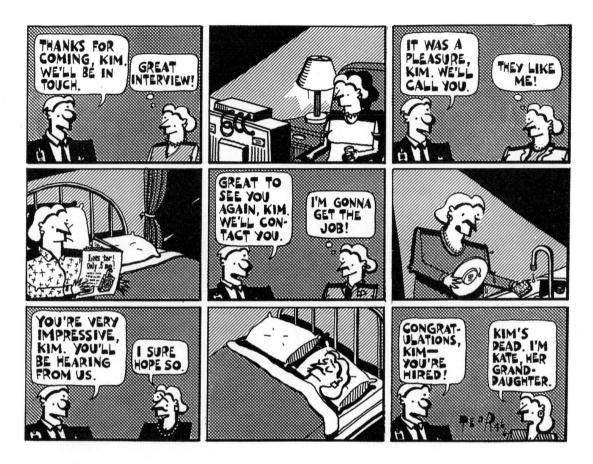

DEBT-FREE IN 30 DAYS OR LESS

Adults between twenty-five and thirty-five years of age currently hold nearly $3 trillion in credit-card debt—more than the total net worth of Vermont and Kazakhstan. "Debt service reduces your financial options. Just think about it—if we still had the cash that was squandered on Ikea furniture and Men At Work albums, we could actually buy Vermont and Kazakhstan back from the Soviets," said Henry J. Owings, an economics professor at Bronx Community College.

I asked the experts what I should do about my $22,000 in student loans and $30,000 in credit-card debt—standard obligations for an American about to turn thirty-four.

"I would apply for *more* credit cards," said Mojave. "You can put the student-loan debt on a new Discover card and live interest-free for a month," he said. "Then you roll over that same amount the following month onto an Optima card. Take just ten minutes each month to fill out a credit application,

and you'll never need to repay a penny of that loan."

What about the $30,000 in credit-card debt? The consultants agreed: Use bad checks to pay off the credit cards, then cut them up. "Afterward, you just call up Amex and Visa and tell them you lost your cards ten years ago and that you don't know anything about those charges," they told me in unison.

REAL ESTATE

These days, the only way an American who doesn't own a politician can get a decent tax deduction is to purchase a home. However, rampant Boomer-driven real estate speculation, stagnant Xer wages, and stringent credit requirements have driven the average age of first-home ownership from twenty-four in 1981 to whatever age the youngest Boomer happens to be at the time (now thirty-seven). How can a savvy Xer bridge the gap between rent slavery and his or her first piece of Don MacLean's famous "American Pie"?

"Today's young people are often unwill-

ing to make concessions to reality," says Poisson. "For instance, you can currently buy a hundred-acre lot, complete with a perfectly adorable farmhouse, for just $33,000 in rural southeastern Ohio. Granted, there aren't any jobs for hundreds of miles. But for a young couple willing to make that commute to Chicago or Boston, where there are plenty of employment opportunities, it's a perfect solution."

Aside from cartographic flexibility, advisers recommend using your imagination to obtain financing. Poisson had trouble qualifying for his first home. Then he hit upon an innovative solution: Remembering that he shared his name with his father, Dartanian Poisson Sr., he went to his father's bank and cleaned out the old man's accounts with the stroke of a pen. The older Poisson died shortly thereafter, and Poisson Jr. inherited what remained of his estate.

"Of course, I miss my dad sometimes," says Poisson. "But financial independence means never having to say you're sorry."

Business as Usual (Redux)

NEW YORK (Agence France-Poisson)—New York City Mayor Rudolph Giuliani and real estate developer Donald Trump have unveiled a $75 billion project to privatize Manhattan's Central Park.

Under the plan described today, the famous 153-square-block enclosure will be leased to Mr. Trump for ninety-nine years at a rent of one dollar per year. In return, Trump will construct Trump Park Garden City Towers, a completely privatized "city within a city" composed of hundreds of luxury high-rise condominiums and office buildings. Manhattan's numbered-grid street configuration will be extended through the park. For instance, the Avenue of the Americas, which now terminates at the southern border of the park at 59th Street, will continue north until it meets Lenox Avenue at 110th Street in Harlem.

"It was an outrage to allow hundreds of billions of dollars of prime Manhattan real estate to go to waste so some self-centered yuppie could walk his damn dalmatian," Mr. Trump said.

City officials say that the rising cost of real estate in the city no longer justifies the luxury of public spaces located in central areas. To replace the land occupied by Trump Park Garden City Towers, New Yorkers who present proof of city residency will still be granted access to a quarter-acre public plaza at the northwest corner of the former Central Park. Trump Plaza Junior, as the new mini-park will be called, will contain a squash court and a concrete dog run.

City consumer advocate Mark Green criticized the fact that Mr. Trump has received a fifty-year tax abatement for the project. "I wasn't even consulted," he complained. "I'm definitely writing a very nasty letter over this one to *The Village Voice.* A very nasty letter."

Please see editorial, "New York Rejoins Civilization," page 312.

10. AMERICA'S SLAVE LABOR

"Fourteen percent of black men are currently or permanently barred from voting because they are in prison or because they have been convicted of a felony."

—The New York Times, *January 30, 1997*

It's damn funny to listen to American politicos complain about China's use of emaciated prisoners to manufacture low-cost products under squalid conditions. In reality, when it comes to slave labor, China has nothing on the United States.

During the last decade alone, American businesses have laid off over a million people. Employees who were lucky enough to be spared from downsizing mania have seen their salaries frozen, their benefits cut back, their retirement plans looted. New hiring for half-decent jobs—the $40,000-plus variety—is virtually nonexistent. Executives preside over a new brand of corporate terrorism under which cowed workers know that they are easily replaceable while their jobs are not. So employees work long hours without asking for overtime pay and perfect the fine art of keeping their mouths shut.

The classic dynamic of labor-management relations prescribes a tug-of-war in which employers demand as much work as they can for as little pay as possible, while workers fight for precisely the opposite conditions. However, decades of government-approved union busting and corporate

Disney pays its Haitian garment workers 30 cents an hour. This may not seem like much.

But, in Haiti, # LESS IS A HELL OF A LOT MORE!

Some people call us cheap for paying Third World workers low wages. But the cost of living in underdeveloped countries is incredibly cheap. $11 a week isn't much here, but by Haitian standards, it's an enormous salary!

But don't take our word for it—Check out what things cost in Haiti:

In the United States, this split-level 3-bedroom home might cost $250,000. But in Haiti, it's just *ten bucks!*

The new Mazda Miata starts at $19,200. But you can find it in Haiti for $1.75!

Clinton and Dole blew $600 million on the 1996 presidential campaign. But you could become the next ruler-for-life* of Haiti for a mere $20,000!

An average bag of groceries will put you out $30. But a Haitian housewife pays $30 to eat for a *lifetime!*

New Yorkers pay $60 a month for premium cable TV. In Haiti, they don't even have cable TV. *Cost: zero!*

*Warning: May be revoked at any time.

THIRD-WORLD WAGES: THERE'S LESS THAN MEETS THE EYE.

sponsorship of politicians, not to mention the sorry fact that many American workers love their companies more than they love themselves, have destroyed every pretense of a fair balance.

Now that they've taken away the company picnic, the year-end bonus, and the dental plan, there's only one more thing to go: the paycheck. But shareholders need not worry—that's next.

PRISON LABOR

As in China, inmates in American prisons are forced to break rocks in road gangs (in Mississippi, for example) or work in sweatshops that make a variety of products—like those Prison Blues jeans that decorate the nation's malls.

In other cases, prison labor is coerced from the internees. During my visit to the maximum-security prison at San Quentin,

California, inmates informed me that roughly a third of them toil in prison workshops at wages ranging from twenty-five cents to a dollar per hour. In exchange for their sub-sub-sub-minimum-wage drudgery, they receive points toward such privileges as single cells and early parole hearings.

Most American voters see nothing wrong with putting convicted criminals to work. Riled by exaggerated anecdotes of country-club jails decked out with five hundred cable-TV channels and fully equipped health clubs, they feel they're fighting back against crime by eliminating prisoner privileges. Never mind that prisoners can't commit crimes against the public once they're in jail or that most of the profits from prison labor goes directly to the private companies that do business with the prison system, while taxpayers see mere pennies on the dollar from these foul little enterprises.

Even in prison, a corporate-style atmosphere of rollbacks prevails. "They're cutting back the number of points you can earn

from working," an incompetent San Francisco bank robber serving a twenty-year term told me. "They've taken away so many benefits that it's getting so that fewer guys want to work."

Inmate-employees don't even receive basic medical care. Incarcerated Americans who've been in the system more than a few years suffer from rotten teeth because they never get access to a dentist. But even if you don't care about the welfare of people who are in the custody of the state, you should care

about this: The increased use of prison labor takes away jobs from law-abiding citizens.

MINIMUM WAGE AND CHILD LABOR

Meanwhile, roughly 6 million Americans, many of them teenagers and young adults, toil at the federal minimum wage, currently set at $5.15 an hour. In some states, teens can receive a "training wage" as low as $4.25. Training for what—indentured servitude?

Conservatives claim that most minimum-wage earners are teens who merely want

extra spending money to purchase CDs and video games, not heads of households trying to support themselves and pay the rent. If so, we, like Voltaire's Candide, must live in the best of all possible worlds. An hourly wage of $5.15 works out to about $800 a month gross for a full-timer. After taxes, that's $550. Sure, in some places it's still possible to pay the rent with $550, but forget about obtaining other luxuries like food, clothing, transportation, or health care.

Even if you accept the argument that minimum-wage earners are all carefree teenagers, how can a supposedly civilized country justify this kind of institutionalized exploitation? Our kids fall asleep in class after closing up the neighborhood Dairy Queen at 3:00 A.M. on school nights. Meanwhile, companies like McDonald's and Burger King ride their cheap slave labor straight to the top of the Big Board.

You have to be a serious twit not to appreciate the irony of high school students, taught that child labor was eliminated at the turn of the century, heading off right after school to work like dogs for slave wages.

It would never occur to Europeans to use children to deliver newspapers or operate cash registers. There, work is considered the provenance of adults; children are permitted to remain children as long as possible.

Here in America, we teach young people we don't care about them in the most efficient way possible: We put them to work. Methods of child labor vary. Middle-class kids sell Girl Scout cookies and cheddar cheese for the marching band. Poor kids push crack, but it's all the same thing: coerced capitalism to benefit adults.

Low wages are merely one repugnant aspect of the practice—the working conditions are terrible as well. When I was thirteen, four of my toes got seriously frostbitten while I delivered copies of the now-defunct *Dayton Journal-Herald* for two hours during a ferocious blizzard. For this I earned a grand total of $20 a week. But I got off easy—mass murderer John Wayne Gacy started his career by killing his paperboy.

And my friend Cole, who at sixteen slaved away in a polyester uniform at a Richmond, Virginia, burger joint, was held up and shot at by a late-night robber. Not only did he *not* receive a bonus or promotion for risking his life in the line of deep-frying duty, he was working for a laughable $2.90 an hour.

America needs a new Emancipation Proclamation, one that ends child labor, ceases exploiting prisoners, and forces em-

ployers to pay a living wage for work. Children have the right to their childhoods, and adults have the right not to compete against kids for kids' wages. It is inhumane and unconscionable that the world's richest country would gleefully exploit its own children for a few upticks on the Dow Jones Industrial Average.

Conventional wisdom—that kids don't have rights because they don't vote—doesn't explain the fact that American adults eat their young. After all, most adults don't vote either!

II. A SPROCKET IN SATAN'S BULLDOZER

"No one is innocent."
—*Sid Vicious, 1977*

I t was a scam from the beginning, starting with my job interview. Peter-the-Assistant-Trust-Officer peered over my résumé at me in a conference room twenty-three floors above Park Avenue and asked me about the blank space where my college graduation date would have appeared had I spent my college years in class instead of the top-floor lounge at Danceteria. He simply asked, "You did graduate, didn't you? This position requires a bachelor's degree, you know."

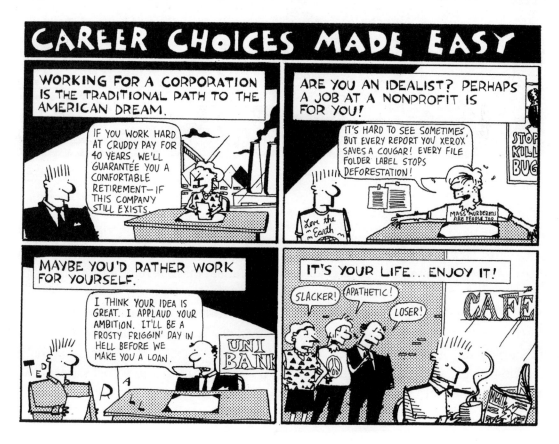

If this were a scene in the movies, I would have started sweating a lot and the room would have spun around me, but up there above Grand Central Station in an office cluttered with enough corporate-bond tombstones to build a split-level Lucite house, all I could think about was that I needed a job that didn't involve deep-frying and scraping the fat off the gas grill at four in the morning. So I muttered, "Uh, yeah." I'm not sure if he heard me.

Fortunately, the question never came up again.

The fact that I was desperate enough to lie to get an administrative assistant job says a lot about my state of mind at the time, but it was by no means the whole story. I was twenty-two years old, a college dropout living in $850-a-month squalor in south Harlem, pulling down $8,500 a year as a trader/trainee at Bear Stearns & Co. I was living the downscale version of the Wall Street

INFANTILE PARALYSIS

WHEN WE LAY OFF PEOPLE, WE FIRE OUR CUSTOMERS.

AND OUR INCOME PLUNGES.

IF WE KEEP OUR EMPLOYEES, OUR PROFITABILITY SUFFERS.

AND OUR COMPETITORS EAT US ALIVE.

WHAT A CONUNDRUM! I'M TOTALLY STUCK.

ME TOO.

MAYBE WE SHOULD GIVE OURSELVES ENORMOUS RAISES?

GOOD COMPROMISE.

scenario, complete with an all-male office, stacks of blinking Quotrons, and an occasional broker getting arrested or pitching dead into his morning scrambled eggs. Only Darryl Hannah and a real salary were missing to complete the picture.

I didn't really mind my role as one of thousands of sweaty guys barking out stock quotes through ten phones at once, scribbling out hundreds of buy/sell tickets an hour, and going home after dark so often I forgot what daylight looked like. Despite my good breeding, I didn't have any moral qualms about working for a boss whose hiring policy was "No blacks, no broads." I was there to pay off a bit of the back rent, not to change the world. And if I got the job at the Industrial Bank of Japan Trust Company, my salary would double to $17,500.

The mid-1980s were supposedly good for people like me, white college-educated stockbrokers, but actually I was a white-

collar impostor. I moved millions of dollars a day and wore a suit, but that was as close as I came to living the life. I was moonlighting as a cabby, earning the same $314.29 in two all-night shifts driving around the boroughs that I got from Bear after taxes every two weeks. It was only a matter of time before something gave.

ROAD TO RUIN

As it turned out, my interview at IBJ had gone well. After temping for three months at the American Institute of Physics, which publishes science magazines, I landed a second interview. I scored a black Brooks Brothers suit jacket at a flea market for ten bucks, procured used policemen's shoes from an Army-Navy store, and stole my burnout roommate's dark blue pants. Black and blue was always a JFK favorite, so it was good enough for me.

Few Americans have heard of it, but at the time IBJ was the second largest bank in Japan and the closest thing that country had to the Federal Reserve Bank. Founded in 1904, it is considered extremely conservative and prestigious, and one of the hardest institutions to get hired by. It has dozens of branches and representative offices that span the globe from Kuala Lumpur to Rome. They never advertise: they're obscure, and that's just the way they like it. They also take accounts that even less principled lenders like Chase Manhattan and Citibank won't touch.

I spent an uneventful year in the bank's trust department, proofreading trust indentures and letters of credit. One moment that broke the monotony was when a vice president wrote himself an

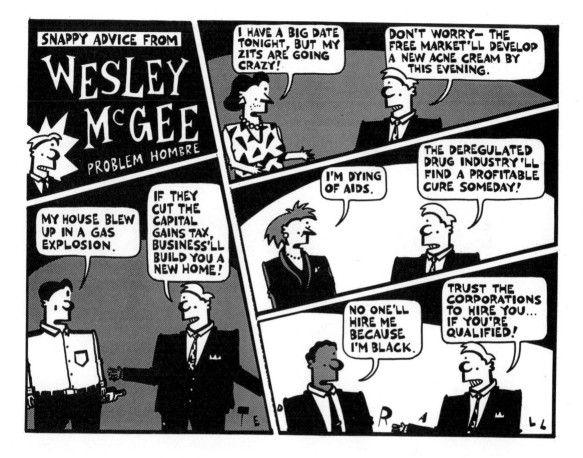

$8 million check out of a client's account and disappeared. As usual in cases like this, they decided to let it go rather than look like morons in the press.

I started to make a name for myself by collecting money from long-overdue accounts. During that time my boss noticed my talent for dealing with problem companies, and within a year I had become IBJ's unofficial pit bull.

Officers would come to me with companies that had defaulted on loans, and I always got them to pay by using my repo-man tactics. At a bank with hundreds of surly Third World borrowers, this proved to be a valuable skill.

FUN WITH MERCURY POISONING

When I got promoted to trust administrator in 1987, I inherited the notorious Albras account. Albras is the state-owned aluminum company of Brazil, principally engaged in strip-mining for tin, zinc, and aluminum in the central Amazon basin.

They build special train lines from the Atlantic coast to the interior to move the stuff, straight through the rain forest. Their work sites look like one of those 1950s epic films set in the time of the pharaohs, with hundreds of worker ants scrambling on their hands and knees in muddy pits for a few cruzeiros a day.

In a carefully considered move made in the midst of a night of overpriced food and sake, IBJ lent Albras a half-billion dollars in 1981. Regrettably, they had never bothered to get the Brazilians to sign a loan agreement. This was a big mistake. Legally speaking, the money was a gift.

Three guys from Brazil would come up to New York every other Friday, ostensibly to negotiate the loan agreement after the fact. But despite six years of "negotiations," zero progress had been made.

This situation was hardly unusual. IBJ also lent $200 million to a Japanese-American joint venture called Alaska Lumber & Pulp without a loan agreement. ALP had never made a payment, as it had lost money every year due to the depressed price of paper. That was in 1959, when Ike was still president, and no one even pretended to ask for the money anymore.

So when the government of Brazil announced that they were going to default on their interest payments to international banks in order to alleviate poverty in 1988, neither my boss nor I bought it. I called up one of the Brazilians:

Me: This is to advise you that, if you fail to make tomorrow's payment, I will authorize a foreclosure on our collateral.

Albras: But we haven't signed the loan agreement yet!

Me: American law says that if you accept the money, you agree to the terms. [A lie.]

Albras: What terms? We don't have an agreement. Anyway, we are a very poor country. Please understand, all the other banks have already agreed. We have to feed the starving children in our streets.

Me: Be that as it may, we will foreclose on our collateral the second you miss a payment. We have a lien on a large public park in São Paulo, and that's where we'll build our new office. Bet that'll go over real well with the starving masses, huh?

Albras: We're too poor. We just can't afford to pay you.

Me: Who do you think you're talking to? Your country is rich. Rich people exploiting poor people doesn't make your country poor. Income redistribution is your problem, not ours. We want our money.

And so we got our money, right on time, every time, while all the American banks were falling all over themselves to write off their "bad" debts to Latin American countries and jacking up checking account fees to pay for their magnanimity.

My experiences with "poor" countries have convinced me that Americans who send donations overseas to fight poverty are delusional fools. With the exception of hopelessly impoverished states like Mali, almost every country on earth possesses sufficient natural resources and industry to adequately support its people. If you don't believe it, check out production levels and banking activity in countries like Mexico. Their poverty stems from the 1 percent of rich assholes who own the whole country and don't give a shit about living in a land of hunger. They keep every stinking peso for themselves while everyone else starves. Those countries don't lack gifts from guilt-ridden Westerners—what they need is a few good bloody revolutions and a lot of dead aristocrats.

Not surprisingly, the Brazilians were incessant in their "demands," finally braying that they wouldn't sign the agreement because they had been insulted by my suggestion that they pay their bills in a timely manner.

My boss ordered me to arrange a weekend for our merry trio of Brazilian government officials at an exclusive $500-an-hour bordello on East 52nd Street—supposedly Henry Kissinger was a frequent patron—to get them to shut up. Although everyone knew that they would mutate into pterodactyls and fly off across Central Park before they ever signed that loan agreement, they insisted on going through the charade of exchanging faxes with specific comments on the document, switching words back and forth, as if there were an actual discussion taking place. Whenever I failed to respond to one of their memos, they'd call my boss and moan that I wasn't working toward a good-faith agreement. For all I know they are still annoying some poor idiot in Trust about that document.

SUNFLOWERS

My mom has always had a print of van Gogh's *Sunflowers* in her living room. I never liked it. Yellow and orange don't do much for me; anyway, it's just a flower arrangement. Besides, according to a hundred-something-year-old French woman who'd known him as a little girl, van Gogh was an asshole.

In spite of that, Yasuda Fire & Marine Insurance Co., Ltd., one of Japan's largest companies, decided to shoot its corporate wad on the real thing and snatched it up for $53.2 million. I wouldn't be at all surprised if they deliberately overpaid to set a new world record for a painting sale (getting into the *Guinness Book* was a big thing to Japanese executives), but since I wasn't involved in that deal, I can't say for certain.

Nonetheless, my boss was dying to see the real thing before it split for some private collection in Japan, so on the pretext of pitching some new deal, we got an appointment to see Yasuda's New York president and, more important, the pricey new painting displayed in his office.

It was February, there was snow on the ground, the sun was shining brightly, and the heat was blasting. This is relevant because Vinnie's orange flowers were hanging over the radiator, in direct sunlight. I made a mental note: After the revolution, nobody will be allowed to own art.

YOUR TAXES AT WORK

In 1988, my boss got transferred from the Corporate

Trust Department to Loan Department No. 2 (Japanese Corporate Section). I followed him shortly thereafter and became a loan administrator in the bank's division that was devoted to loans to American subsidiaries of Japanese corporations.

Our customers were mostly auto-parts and chemical companies that wanted to open plants in the United States, especially in the Midwest. I was assigned to research locations for our clients to build their facto-

ries and to negotiate tax abatements and other incentives with the relevant cities and counties once they had decided on a spot. I naturally came upon this responsibility as the only fluent English-language male speaker in the department. There were two female loan administrators, but they were strictly clerical—Japanese companies tend to be unabashedly sexist and racist.

First, I'd run a comparison of employment statistics of towns in areas that were

convenient for the company, taking into consideration criteria like being near a highway or one of their suppliers. Target communities would have high unemployment, low wages, no unions, and lax environmental enforcement. It is amazing to see how states compete against one another with brochures like *Tennessee: A Right-to-Work State with Minimal Union Activity!* These officials, whose salaries come from taxpaying workers, have no interest in seeing their citizens earn a living wage.

All they want is more jobs, regardless of the cost or the quality of the jobs.

Then I'd practice my best local twang, the intensity of which was directly proportional to how far south I was calling. I'd call the three top candidates for a plant and let them fight like weasels over a few low-wage jobs. Once, when a chemical company needed a fairly educated workforce, I called the Economic Development Office of Moraine, Ohio, a stone's throw from where I grew up:

Me: Hi! My name is Ted Rall and I'm a loan officer at the Industrial Bank of Japan in New York. [I'd say *Nyew Yerk.*] I have a client that wants to build a twenty-million-dollar plant in Moraine. They'll be hiring fifty people. [Untrue—it was probably more like 20, but by the time the plant was finished, it would be too late to complain.] Can you waive your property taxes?

Moraine: Sure, we can do that, no problem. We normally waive property taxes and utilities for ten years. [There goes a few mil-

lion for the local schools.]

Me: What about roads? My client's plant needs an access road and its own entrance to Interstate 75.

Moraine: We can build a ramp for your client. [For about $5 million. Oh well, the rest of the city will have a few more potholes.]

Me: There's a sewage problem—there are no lines on the property. We'll need you to pay for them.

Moraine: Okay. [If a private citizen built a house there, he'd have to pay for the hookup himself.]

Me: Also, many of their employees are Japanese. Can you establish a Japanese-language school for their kids? [I'm going for the gusto—this one is not that important.]

Moraine: We don't have that.

Me: Tennessee will do that. [True.]

Moraine: I'll look into it. [My client, which enjoys annual profits of more than $150 million, has just saved about $8 million. Should they choose to locate there, maybe they'll buy some lame painting with the extra money.]

Although the company in this particular deal eventually built their plant in another city, this routine goes on every day in every community in the United States. (In my experience the only state that won't sell its citizens' wages and taxes down the river to whore for some business is Massachusetts. It's not that interested in "economic development.") There are no genuine net benefits to granting concessions to a company to build in your community. You don't collect any taxes, you pay millions to bring roads and sewers to their door, and chances are that they'll leave in less than ten years anyway. On the other hand, the toxins they leave behind will be around a very long time.

A NEW FAMILY

On April Fools' Day, 1989, IBJ made the mistake of promoting me to loan officer. (Raises were always announced on April 1, and annual bonuses were issued on Pearl Harbor Day. Who says bankers don't have a sense of humor?) It was a big jump: I got $36,000 plus a month's bonus (the peak of my earnings), four weeks' vacation, and signing authority to execute indentures and wire-transfer money. My boss kept complimenting me (and he was serious): "For an American, you are very intelligent." Not bad for someone without a college degree.

The largest deal I worked on as an officer was Nippon Mining Co., Ltd.'s 1989 acquisition of Gould, Inc., a Cleveland-based defense contractor, for $1.1 billion. The Department of Defense doesn't permit foreign companies to own defense contractors, so as part of the arrangement, the separate defense-related subsidiaries had to be spun off and sold as separate companies. As in all leveraged buy-out transactions, the acquired companies got stuck with the borrowed debt for being purchased while the profits went to the old management.

One of these spinoffs was a Fort Lauderdale computer-hardware company that employed 2,400 people. It was a very profitable business, but once it had to pay for the golden parachutes for the bigwigs who had sold it, it was screwed. They laid off half the staff one day after the purchase; within weeks they were boarded shut.

There were countless subsidiary transactions to the Gould deal, which kept us busy for almost a year, but the one that caught my attention was the $330 million revolving line of credit.

It's fairly difficult to embezzle from an investment bank because most transactions are closely monitored. There are frequent statements to the customers, controls on withdrawals, and checkpoints for money to travel through before it can be sent anywhere, even by wire transfer.

Nippon Mining was different. Every

My plan was to wait for a month when Nippon Mining didn't want to increase their loan. On that day, I would authorize a direct wire transfer of $100 million to an account in Luxembourg, which would be immediately transferred out to another European city, then to another, over and over during the next few days. For this, I needed conspirators.

Norm S. was a twenty-three-year-old loan administrator and Emily C. was an

month, the client would call to roll over a $330 million loan. Sometimes they would ask for an extra $100 million, in which case we'd send them a wire transfer, or they'd repay $100 million. Because of the lackadaisical structure of the loan, we sent only one statement a month. I had signing authority on Nippon Mining.

I guess I'm just a bad person, but I became preoccupied with the thought of pulling off the biggest theft in banking history.

operations clerk. I took both of them out for drinks at Rockefeller Center's opulent Rainbow Room, and by the third round, they were convinced.

I would sign the wire transfer order and give it to Norm, who would then give it to our favorite operations person, Emily, who would then send the money. Although most U.S. banks have "correspondent bank" relationships with New York banks to send money out of the country, New York banks, being in New York, don't. The correspondent system is very effective at checking for unauthorized transfers, except for this omission.

There was no one to cross-check our actions—we were all supposed to cross-check one another. The system relied on the three classes of employees (officer, administrator, and clerk) not socializing, much less conspiring to run off together with the bank's money. Nippon Mining wouldn't get a

there and bankers do not cooperate with the authorities to trace funds. In the meantime, Norm and I would keep working as if everything were normal. Then, in a few weeks, over a long weekend, we would vanish.

No one would have ever known until it was too late. Personally, I planned to go to a country like Libya that doesn't have an extradition treaty with the U.S. What's the point of stealing all that money to go on the run?

statement that month—Emily was in charge of sending them out, so she would intercept it. They might notice in about three weeks, but that gave us ample time to be long gone.

Immediately after the wire transfer, Emily would take her vacation and fly to Europe, where she would recover the money by opening three numbered, unnamed accounts at banks in Luxembourg. She would transfer the money incrementally one piece at a time. Unlike the Swiss, no one ever asks questions

Norm wanted plastic surgery and a new identity. (In his case, that would have been best.) Our problem was Emily. In the end, a mere month before the heist of the century was to take place, she took Norm and me out for drinks and told us that she couldn't go through with our plan because she would never be able to see her family again.

Norm tried to reason with her. "You could bring them to wherever you are!"

I suggested, "You could travel under an

assumed identity back to the U.S., just like Dr. Mengele, who used to send postcards postmarked from Manhattan to the Jewish Defense League in Brooklyn. Besides, they'd be too embarrassed to put your face in the papers."

No amount of reasoning worked. She simply couldn't bear the thought of the big adieu to Mom and Dad.

I couldn't imagine anyone's parents being both irreplaceable and immovable. "Shit, with thirty-three million, you can buy yourself another family!"

Thus ended my flirtation with white-collar crime. I am certain that my plan would have worked, not despite the scale involved but because of it. No thief has ever been that audacious, except for some First Chicago employees who tried the same thing in 1993. They got tripped up by the correspondent bank system in New York. Too bad I wasn't working in New York at the time—I could have hooked them up.

I can't say that I never extracted any benefit out of my five years as an investment banker. For example, my boss and I and two lawyers once got shitfaced on obscenely pricey 1960s wine at Le Cirque (at the time the most expensive restaurant in New York), all courtesy of IBJ.

Aside from such debauchery, I met some surprisingly cool people. One of my clients, a middle-aged chief financial officer from an electronics company who looked boring as hell, turned out to have been living in a car containing all of his possessions just three years earlier. There was a senior vice president at Shearson who graduated with an engineering degree, played rhythm guitar in an East Village punk group, and ripped clothes from her pregnant body in bizarre performance pieces. One of the operations clerks in my department once stole a book of company taxi vouchers, all as good as cash, and took corporate taxis all over the Eastern seaboard from Cape Cod to Florida, all at my bank's expense. Now and then he'd call us from some resort, laughing hysterically. He made me glad to be alive.

But in the end, working within the system is not the answer. The structure is so much bigger and more powerful than anyone inside it that it eats them alive. You have to be as far away from the evil machinery of soulless greed as possible if you want to slow it down or at least avoid its clutches. During World War II, a Jewish member of the German Resistance successfully managed to join the SS in order to try to effect change from within the Nazi system. After witnessing countless horrors against his people, he realized he was not only powerless, but also complicitous. He shot himself in 1943.

12. GEN XPLOITATION

"No matter where you end up in the business world, you'll likely be teamed with
or report to a baby boomer, those demanding workaholics born between 1946 and 1964.
Trying to avoid their bossy ways is an option, but learning to function
within their guidelines is a smarter career move."
—*"How to Succeed in a 'Boomer' World, College Edition,"*
National Business Employment Weekly *(Spring/Summer 1995)*

If you're like most Baby Boomers, you gave up idealism and rock 'n' roll long
ago for middle management and a split-level in a gated community. The
trouble is, those damn acid flashbacks keep turning your assistant vice president into a five-foot-tall purple spitting toad during strategy meetings. Well,
that's *part* of the problem, anyway.

The rest of your problem is those inscrutable Generation X administrative assistants who do all your real work for Honduran garment worker wages. They know they're underpaid and overworked, yet nonetheless they show up every morning, apparently alert and prepared to work. Who knows why they put up with you? What perverse masochism allows humans to function under such dreary conditions? How long will it take before they crack? Will they take it out on you? It's enough to make anyone nervous as hell.

Without these sullen Nez Percé types to make the computer print out those cool window-spreadsheet-whatevers you need to create your reports, your tenuous stewardship of the Domestic Operations Department would surely come to a deafening halt, forcing you to mingle with the vast national unwashed in what's left of the county welfare office, your spouse to seek the counsel of the nearest divorce lawyer, and your well-fed kids into one of those icky public schools. It's an ugly scenario, and the only thing separating your yuppie reality from a downscale future is a crew of sullen glorified secretaries with goatees and disturbing tattoos. Even worse, you need these wage slaves much more than they need you, and what's much, much worse: they know it.

But allowing them to walk around your office tweaks your shadow of a conscience, even though their fashion sense drives you nuts—haven't these people ever heard of chinos and Docksiders?

The first key to understanding your twentysomething employees, many of whom are thirty-seven years old, is to accept that they hate you. Oh, sure, they smile blankly at you, ask about your kids'

college prospects, and compliment you on your new Jeep Cherokee. That's when you're looking.

The second you're out during lunch, trolling the mall for the new live double CD by Earth, Wind & Fire, your twenty-six-year-old intern with the clunky black shoes and the twenty-four-year-old clerk with that thing in her left eyelid and the thirty-three-year-old junior assistant associate with the thin tie from the fifties meet at the local Starbucks to plot your demise.

Sharie Hanes (not her real name), a twenty-nine-year-old junior assistant at a New Haven insurance company, admits to offing her first Boomer boss about one year ago. "My manager was this gross ex-hippie," Hanes said, rolling her eyes like the ball in a roulette wheel. "Larry was always talking about socially responsible business—you know, 'doing well by doing good,' and all that P.C. Boomer crap. Meanwhile the guy was paying me twelve bucks an hour, without overtime. The medical plan he got for us

never covered you when you actually went to visit the doctor.

"So one day during lunch I went out to the parking lot and loosened the front wheel nuts on his four-by-four. It drove me crazy; nothing happened for days and I was beginning to think I'd messed up. But that Saturday, he was driving with his wife and prep-school spawn to the factory-outlet mall. According to the news, he hit a bridge abutment doing about sixty," Hanes recalls, smiling thinly.

Rather than promote a Gen Xer to fill the now-defunct Larry's position, Hanes's employer chose to hire another Boomer from outside the company. "Of course, she's no different from Larry. She spews that 'team player' rhetoric all the time, but then she signs her name to my work. But I have a plan to deal with her. I got a bunch of thermometers on sale from Wal-Mart and broke them all into a bowl. I've been dropping tiny balls of mercury into her coffee ever since she

denied my extra week of unpaid vacation."

Hanes's gericide is not unusual. According to the Denver-based consulting firm Effective Exploitation Enterprises, Gen Xers will murder more than thirty thousand Boomer bosses this year. With so many managers paying for their hiring decisions with a permanent vacation, shouldn't you learn to do without twentysomething employees?

Of course not. Gen Xers are a vital source of high-quality labor at bargain-base-

ment prices. These ex–latchkey kids are self-loathing, highly leveraged with student loans, and have low expectations. Having entered the job market after you Boomers had taken all the good jobs, even Harvard grads consider themselves fortunate to perform eighty hours a week of soul-crushing data entry at $18,000 a year, all so you can afford to give your daughter a brand-new Miata for her Sweet Sixteen. They understand how to put your company on that

World Wide Super Information Highway Internet thing, how to produce desktop-publishing stuff, and how to get the jammed paper out of location A3 of the Xerox machine. They've learned not to expect job security, a pension plan, or decent medical benefits. They're too alienated to unionize. So why go all the way to Nanjing when you can hire budget-priced labor right here in America? If you dazzle these image sluts with vacuous charm, they'll forget all about hack-ing you to pieces, blowing you away with a shotgun, or injecting you with some toxin. Xers are surly, but they're a CEO's wettest dream: an overeducated underclass!

Here are a few pointers on how to keep your Xer drones in check:

Promote style over substance. These people grew up on trash television culture. For them, image is everything. So don't fret if they won't dress appropriately. These people

hate wearing ties and stockings more than they hate you—and their hatred of you is considerable. So let them wear their weird tattoos and pierced-navel-exposing shirts, and they'll never pester you for a raise!

Invite them to meetings. Nothing angers an Xer more than feeling left out of the loop. Ask their opinions about new policies. Obviously you'll make the real decisions with your fellow Boomers once the young 'uns are

out of the room, but it never hurts to make them feel important. Quote to memorize: "We argued for hours over this one. I fought for you, because you were right, but the other bastards conspired against me."

Provide training. Xers know they'll be the first to go the next time the shareholders squawk, so they're always looking for new skills to take with them when they leave. Ask them to train each other—this

POMO ENGLISH GLOSSARY
Terms You'll Need to Manage the Younger Set

Are you a Baby Boomer who sometimes has difficulty understanding the under-forty set? Do your references to the Chicago 7 and "Ellessdee" sometimes fall flat? There's nothing quite as embarrassing as not "getting" it, but don't worry, be cool, chill out—here are the essential terms that will allow you to "pass" with young American adults. Remember—dropping these terms, which typically represent nostalgic moments in mass pop culture (either earnest or sarcastic) is sufficient. **There's no need to comprehend their meanings.** Memorize and apply them at random; soon you'll communicate, exploit, and seduce Generation Xers at will!

TV Shows

The Six Million Dollar Man
The A-Team
Baywatch Nights
The Brady Bunch
Beverly Hills 90210
Chico and the Man
Dallas
Donahue
Friends

Hollywood Squares
Knight Rider
Room 222
Sanford and Son
Speed Racer
Starsky & Hutch
T. J. Hooker
The Rockford Files
Ultraman

Example of Proper Use
"Oh, God—remember the *Donahue* show when it was still in Dayton? Man, that was the best!" (Smile knowingly.)

Music

A Flock of Seagulls
Abba
AC/DC
Aerosmith
Chemical Brothers
Human League
Judas Priest
Kiss
Lynyrd Skynyrd
Men Without Hats

Nirvana
Partridge Family
Public Enemy
Ramones
Rolling Stones (circa Tattoo You)
Run-DMC
Sid Vicious (solo)
Stereolab
Tony Orlando & Dawn

Example of Proper Use
"I don't care what anyone says—Frankie Goes to Hollywood was great! I mean, of course they sucked—but in a cool way!" (Grin ironically.)

Movies

Alien
Bad Lieutenant
Blade Runner
  (the director's cut)
Carrie
Dawn of the Dead
Drop Dead Fred
Eddie and the Cruisers
Fast Times at Ridgemont High
Ferris Bueller's Day Off
Heathers
Jaws 3-D
Meatballs
Muriel's Wedding

My Life as a Dog
Night of the Hunter
Pink Flamingos
Police Academy 4
Police Academy 5
Pretty in Pink
Pulp Fiction
Repo Man
Risky Business
Rock 'n' Roll High School
The Shining
Sixteen Candles
Slacker
Terminator

Example of Proper Use

"Remember *Splash*? 'Lesbian no more,' indeed!" (Über-Boomer Tip: If you don't know a line from the relevant film, feel free to make one up. This makes your Gen X listener feel stupider than [s]he really is, thus propelling your social status onward and upward!)

Personalities

Brad Pitt
Christian Slater
Eddie Vedder
Harry Dean Stanton
  (honorary)
Ice T
Jello Biafra
Kevin Smith
Kurt Cobain

Kurt Loder
Pamela Anderson Lee
Parker Posey (probationary)
Perry Farrell
Quentin Tarantino
Ricki Lake
The Coen Brothers
Tipper Gore
Winona Ryder

Example of Proper Use

(It helps to mention obscure figures here.) "Did you hear? Boy George is marrying the woman who sued George C. Scott for sexual harrassment! Cool, huh?" (Insert insouciant wink here.)

costs no money, takes no effort, and doesn't give your competitors an advantage when they hire them.

Be cruel to be kind. Xers appreciate honesty. So, when you hire them, tell them with a straight face: No raises. No bonuses. No promotions. They'll stay with you forever; after all, you were honorable with them from the start.

Offer useless retirement plans. More than anything else, Xers crave security in a constantly changing world. Be sure to give your employees an exceptionally good company-retirement package, but make it one in which they'd have to work for ten years before becoming vested. Obviously you'll lay them off before they ever collect a cent, but they'll think that you're just groovy!

Use positive reinforcement. Let your staffers know when they've done a good job. Used "Employee of the Month" plaques only cost a buck each. Up-front displays of your appreciation for work that's earning you big bucks are free, and nothing is stopping you from filling up their personnel files with slanderous memos, even (especially!) if they don't deserve it.

Bring in the comfy chair. Unlike other employees, your Xer workers won't be in much of a rush to breeze out the door at 5:00 P.M. Why should they fight rush hour just to get back to their one-bedroom walk-ups in the slums? But you can keep them at work even longer with low-cost measures to make your workplace comfortable. Stock the fridge with sodas and snacks. Buy ergonomically correct office furniture. And, if you're willing to install a stereo and shower facilities, you'll extract a twenty-four-hour workday!

Know the lingo. An occasional savvy reference to popular culture may not make you one of "them"—anyway, who wants to sleep on a futon on the floor in some cold-water flat with bars on the windows?—but it may make you understood. Examples: "Global positioning is like Courtney Love!" "Tech Support is the *Feeling Minnesota* of this RFP." "What would Marcia Brady do about the audit?"

In this profit-sensitive economy, you just can't afford not to make the most of your Gen X employees. Train this army of wage slaves well, practice your ersatz hipness, and remember, the "X" stands for "exploitation"!

13. RELATIONSHIP TIPS FOR THE SEXLESS

"I can't stand watching you fall apart. That's why I'm dumping you."
—*My college girlfriend, 1984*

As the grizzled veteran of three dozen relationships, including a dozen of the serial-monogamy variety, I am at least as well qualified to dole out advice in matters of the heart as any number of syndicated sex-advice columnists, many of whom have become born-again virgins. Moreover, unlike most advisers on matters of the heart, I have never encountered any relationship that was truly happy.

I understand the sad, terrible truth: People put up with each other in order to ensure a steady supply of sex. Eventually, the sex goes away, of course, but by then senility has begun its insidious progression, and it doesn't really matter. I know these things. After all, my parents hated each other, and whatever is true about me must apply to everyone under thirty-five, right?

To read magazines and Web sites is to believe that the sexual revolution is over, that AIDS has put an end to promiscuity, and that the Boomers used up all the good times. But I know better.

More often than not, sex is unsafe as hell. It's all most people—particularly the pre-married set—think about, ever. The sexual revolution is with us still; it's just a little more furtive, and therefore that much more fun. Serial monogamy has replaced the rotating-bed commune, but the confusions are the same. It's in that spirit that I offer the following observations, using a format blatantly pilfered from those very same sex therapists.

So, Ted. Have you tasted the fruits of a variety of sexual experiences? Have you ever been with another man, for example?

—NOT GAY IN GALLIPOLIS, OHIO

Um, no. As a longtime man myself, I know enough about the gender's grooming and mating habits not to find myself drawn to another man's charms. However, and I'm telling the truth here: I do have a close friend who's trying to hook up with a bonobo. Draw your own conclusions.

My lover and I are seriously into bondage. We have a question. Is it politically gauche to set up a

scenario under which the dom dresses in full SS uniform and uses electric torture devices to torment a victim, asking the sub where the Resistance is hiding, etc.? We're both Jewish.

—STURMFÜHRER AND LOVING IT

So you're saying that you purposefully re-create horrific Holocaust-based history for sexual arousal? Personally, I see nothing wrong with what two consenting adults decide to consent to, but I would have some problems with your scenario's details. For instance, are we talking the dress uniform of the SS, which was black, or the field gray? Field gray would probably be more appropriate here. Furthermore, it is very important to get all the correct accessories—Iron Cross, epaulets, etc.—to go with the uniform. Historical inaccuracies can lead to impotence and other sexual difficulties, not to mention the ever-present dysfunction of revisionism.

I'm seventeen, but I'm still a virgin. Is there something wrong with me?

—UGLY AND INSECURE PERSON WHO WANTS TO
BLOW HIS HEAD OFF AND SCATTER BRAIN PARTICLES ALL
OVER THE COUCH, THE FLOOR, AND THE CEILING

Yes, there is. According to government statistics, everyone whose face is more attractive than the average knee has enjoyed delicious, succulent sex by the age of sixteen. Let me make myself perfectly clear: You are a loser. I myself, however, had to wait until college, but that's different because things worked out in the long run. Know what I mean?

My boyfriend and I are about to move in together. My parents are having a shitfit. We need to save money on rent, but my mom says it's immoral. How should I handle my mother?

—LIVING IN NEAR SIN

Morals, as Kierkegaard (a guy you've never been forced to read in school) says, are subjective. Your mom is off her rocker—if she's so concerned about it, why doesn't she pay your damn rent? On the other hand, living together rarely works out. Statistically, few marriages that follow living together last. You have all the disadvantages of marriage (you can't bring dates home) and all the disadvantages of singlehood (no commitment, the other person can walk whenever you have a fight). If the rent's so bad, consider moving to Portland. The rent's cheap there, and it's a pretty cool place for a city that's not Seattle.

What contraceptives are best?

— ZERO TAX DEDUCTIONS

First of all, let's get one thing straight: You probably aren't going to use any form of contraception much, with the possible exception of one-night stands, and even then, you'll probably forget to bring it. On the other hand, there are few acts more reprehensible than bringing children into the world as an accidental by-product of two margaritas and a six-pack. In other words, there is no practical solution.

I have these funny bumps on my genitals. Could it be . . . ?

— BRAILLE CROTCH IN FORT WAYNE

Yeah, Bumpy, it could be. But it could also be acne. How can you tell? Herpes blisters are clear; zits look like zits, with yellow pus. If you have glowing green zit-blisters, however, call your vet.

I hear there's a cure for herpes. True?

— NOT THE SAME PERSON AS ABOVE

I don't know. Could be true. Could be false. All I can say is that a close friend had the Big H for years, courtesy of a notable rock star's girlfriend. He responded to one of those ads on the back page of his local alternative weekly newspaper, flew down to Tijuana three times, each visit six weeks apart, and was administered some experimental Mexican witches' brew through a big turkey-baster type thing. That was over three years ago, and he claims that he hasn't experienced an outbreak since. On the other hand, he could be lying.

I'm terrified of meeting my boyfriend's parents. How should I handle it?

— PREGNANT WITH TWINS

You should be scared shitless. I'm scared just thinking about it, and I'm married now. Most people's parents are racist, sexist Republican psychopaths who think their kids deserve mates so perfect that they don't exist. Your best course of action is to tie on a few drinks before the main event. Don't talk much; it's especially vital not to discuss politics or foreign films. Just smile and say "Uh-huh" and "That's right" a lot. I'd like to say that everything will go fine, but it won't.

My partner refuses to perform oral sex on me, yet I accommodate her needs in that area without question, above and beyond the call of duty, whether or not I'm asked. Is it unreasonable for me to feel resentful?

—TONGUE SLAVE

Get over it. Sheez—people are starving to death on the streets, various countries on the African subcontinent have imploded into civil war, and all you're worried about is getting your crotch slathered with saliva. I hope you die.

What about unplanned pregnancy?

—JUST CURIOUS

There are so many inefficient and impracticable forms of contraception available that this should never, ever happen to an intelligent person, and it doesn't. But it would make a great name for a band. Really. Think about it.

I'm dating a woman from a different ethnic background. Not only do we get hassled on the streets, but my relatives are bothering me about it too. **—LIBERAL IN LUBBOCK**

The rate of interracial marriage tells you a lot about how accepted a minority group is by mainstream white America. For instance, 60 percent of Asian-Americans marry outside their race; only 0.6 percent of African-Americans do. No wonder the model minority doesn't live in the projects. To hell with the idiots on the streets; your courage is helping make this country a decent place to live in. You don't owe an explanation to anyone for your love. You may, however, want to consider buying a gun.

I've started seeing a woman, and her birthday is coming up. I'm thinking of giving her a bottle of balsamic vinegar for the big event. What do you think?

—MR. CONSIDERATE

Find a tall building. Take the elevator to the top floor. Find the stairs and go up to the roof. Walk to the edge of the building. Close your eyes. Keep walking.

CONFIDENTIAL TO CAN'T GET LAID: Sex isn't for everyone. Lots of people never have sex. Many people don't even like sex. Maybe you're not supposed to have sex anyway. How do you know you deserve sex? Perhaps you're one of those people who are supposed to grow old and shriveled, alone and worthless, the kind of person who wouldn't be any worse off if they'd never been born. Don't rule out the possibility. On the other hand, I could be talking about someone not like you at all, if you know what I mean. Right?

14. POMO FRIENDSHIP

"Robert and I can go years without seeing each other. Then when we meet again, we can just pick up like nothing's happened."
—*Famous friendship lie*

"I like bananas," one gorilla tells another in an old *Far Side* cartoon. "Of course, we all do . . . but I really, really, *really* like bananas." That's the way I feel about friendship. Everyone likes to have friends, but when you're an only child raised by a single mother, you learn to really, really, *really* like friendship.

There's oodles of delicious irony in the state of friendship at this turn of the century. Thanks to modern technology and the cheap foreign labor that makes modern technology possible, never before have there existed so many ways to reach out and touch someone. You can send a virtual greeting card as an e-mail file attachment, but then you're missing actual hanging-out time while your modem sits frozen for hours. Forms of communication designed to simplify our lives transform the simplest task into a living hell, making it nearly impossible to maintain what used to be called friendship.

Just last summer, for instance, I attempted to arrange an evening of beer consumption with a guy who had offered me a job doing Web editing. Although the gig never materialized, John e-mailed me with the idea that we meet for drinks. The next day I e-mailed *him* that his plan sounded like great fun, and asked when he wanted to do this. The next day he e-mailed me back, suggesting the following Monday night. That night some computer geek at Network Solutions, Inc., the company that maintains the master domain-name directory for the Internet, ignored an automated alarm that was trying to tell him that domain addresses were getting garbled. My friend's e-mail then bounced back as "undeliverable," so he re-sent it the next day. Since Monday is my deadline night, I suggested either Tuesday or Thursday as alternatives. That was on Friday. He left town for the weekend, as all good patriotic New Yorkers do during the summer, but he got back to me Sunday night with his choice: Thursday. I replied to his e-mail twelve hours later to confirm, but asked where and what time he wanted to

meet. It has now been six months since John suggested that we hang out. One of us will die before we get to have those beers.

It's unbelievably cruel that at a time like this, when divorce and long-distance families have made camaraderie more important to our collective sanity than ever before, technology is making it nearly impossible to get to know anyone. Since we must learn to live in this dismal world, however, it's vital that we understand how the fundamental nature of friendship is evolving. When you meet

someone you don't necessarily hate on sight, you'll need to immediately classify them into the appropriate form of postmodern friendship to ensure proper handling:

Virtual Friend: I have a pre-Copernican view of human relationships. If I'm Earth, my wife is Telstar—someone in close orbit, who knows the vast majority, if not everything, of what I'm doing and thinking. A close friend is a moon, someone in true sync with my life. A virtual friend is Pluto, or Planet X—they're

technically in my orbit, but they're so distant and remote that they might as well live on Alpha Centauri. Virtual friends are more often than not former close friends who moved away or you moved away from, people you talk to out of primordial guilt. They still use inside jokes that you've forgotten about, discuss mutual acquaintances you no longer care about, and tell stories you'd expunged from your personal history. Unfortunately, Internet directories and membership search engines make it incredibly easy for these annoying social relics to contact you. For instance, a former high-school classmate recently tracked me down using the World Wide Web version of the white pages. "I have difficulty reconciling your writing with the guy I went to high school with," he commented. How the hell would he know? We had never been friends in high school. In fact, I thought he hated me. Virtual friends are often your former enemies.

Outer-Orbit Friends: Formerly known as "acquaintances," outer-orbitrons mean different things to different people. Many humans, suffering from a limited capacity to interact meaningfully with other members of their species, enjoy the low-risk, low-maintenance lifestyle, as well as the ersatz popularity, of maintaining a cloud of outer-orbit friends. You hear from these people every few weeks or months. When they do call, you have trouble recognizing their voices. If a decade passes without contact, it's no big deal. Outer-orbit friends have their advantages though, namely as wedding guests and business contacts. They're also insurance that you'll look good at your funeral, what with so many mourners in attendance—unless none of them show up. The greatest peril is that outer-orbit friends often assume that *other* outer-orbiters are covering for them. (Warning: They will often invite you to mass gatherings of other

outer-orbiters, but no matter what, do not go. These are invariably *the most boring people in the entire world.*) I cull my outer-orbit pals (but not the business contacts) every year when I transfer phone numbers over to my new datebook. Aside from parking meters that go to zero the second a car pulls out of the space, one of the most depressing aspects of life is that close friends often become outer-orbit friends. Outer-orbit friends, however, almost never become close friends.

Leftover Friends: Everyone knows people whom he or she met through a now-extinct relationship. They live in the purgatory between inner- and outer-orbit. They know you fairly well, but you wouldn't want to confide your sexual habits to them. Sure, you don't care about That Person anymore, but just the same, you would prefer that they didn't hear anything embarrassing about

you through this "leftover." Still, under other circumstances you might have become true friends.

Intentional Friends: John of the beer e-mail is an example of this new breed. Intentional friends are individuals who really, really, *really* like you, and who you really, really, *really* like, but somehow you can never, ever seem to get it together to hang out. You're both working eighty-five-hour weeks, trying to start bands and zines, coping with the death of your girlfriend's cat, concentrating on getting out of town on weekends in order to stay sane, and your schedules never overlap because neither of you has any spare time whatsoever. You leave voice mails and e-mails that say things like "We'll *definitely* get together soon," and you both know you never will, but it really sucks because you know you have countless things in common that you'd love to share if

you ever had the time—but you don't. I've accumulated several of these intentional friends in the last year. Outer-orbit friends will sometimes masquerade as intentional friends, but you can root them out *by making actual plans*. Two consecutive cancellations are a bad sign.

Close Friends: Aside from CEOs and other welfare leeches, overworked Americans have time for no more than two close friends. You talk to close friends every day or two, see them at least once a week, and tell them things you wouldn't confide to anyone else. They know your dreams, your fears, and your weaknesses. They know when you're lying or exaggerating, but they forgive you nonetheless. They can tell when you're angry or worried without a word being spoken, and in many ways, they make life worth living. Close friends love you for who you are, not for what they want you to be. But, most important, close friends make all the other varieties of friendship unnecessary.

15. BEEN THERE, DONE THAT

"But when a long Train of Abuses and Usurpations, pursuing invariably the same Object, evinces a Design to reduce them under absolute Despotism, it is their Right, it is their Duty, to throw off such Government . . ."
—*The Declaration of Independence*

Most Americans, the ones who pay attention to what's going on in the real world anyway, agree that this country is in a bad way. The government is completely controlled by corporations, the disparity between rich and poor has widened to ludicrous proportions, and the environment is totally ruined.

Ordinary people—the ones who do the work and pay the taxes and die in the wars—have no access to their elected officials. Our virtual democracy offers an absurd "choice" between two nearly identical ideologies—moderate-conservative Democrats and moderate-conservative Republicans. The system doesn't work, and few act as though they would miss it if it went away.

As the simpleminded saying goes, though, you shouldn't simply advocate abolishing a system without offering a clear alter-native. So what alternatives could be considered by Americans looking to replace their ersatz republican democracy? What follows is an overview of other systems of government I found lying around not doing anything.

Socialism. Ever since Lenin's 1,800 barely armed guys bluffed their way into the Kremlin, Marxism has always stood as the most obvious alternative to capitalistic democracy. It's hard to top an ideology based on the idea that as all people are equal, so should everyone's pay be equal, and that powerful notion drove countless revolutions from 1848 until the eighties. Nonetheless, there's no way such egalitarianism could ever catch on in the United States. Conditioned by two centuries of anti-Communist propaganda, founded by Puritan fanatics and fiercely individualist, America is a nation under which poor people want to lower the capital gains tax to prepare for the day when they'll win the lottery.

Parliamentary democracy. This form of government is dominant throughout Europe and elsewhere, yet is scorned by Americans accustomed to their two-party system. The press often points to frequently shifting parliamentary alliances in Italy as proof that it doesn't work. What it really proves is that having twenty-eight parties spanning the political spectrum is simply too complicated for the average American to comprehend. The very same people who would howl in derision at a supermarket that didn't carry clear dishwashing liquid prefer their choices short and sweet. Still, it would address the biggest weakness in our Republocratic Party—a lack of representation for the vast majority of voters.

Fascism. Although goose-stepping went out with Franco, all those uniforms still hold the imagination of many Americans depressed by our atrocious national anthem and lame-ass flag. We could go for the pageantry, the fanfare, the excitement of right-wing totalitarianism, but only for a short time. Eventually we'd kill off all of the scapegoats, and besides, Americans don't like to be told *overtly* what to do: They'd rather absorb the party line by osmosis, through entertainment media. Fascism wouldn't last five years here, and would leave a lot of people—like me—dead.

Anarchy. Basically, this means everyone runs around aimlessly, shouting and setting off car alarms, playing Def Leppard at 4:00 A.M., breeding iguanas because they can, dropping bricks off the freeway overpass—in short, doing whatever they want. Who would pick up the trash? Who would issue dog licenses? Who would declare war against Third World dictators we once armed? No, for all the talk of antigovernment sentiment, Americans like to have someone run things. That's why they don't mind paying 40 percent of their income to take care of stuff like potholes and wars on drugs. If we had to go around doing everything for ourselves, when would we have time to watch TV? It'd never work.

Monarchy. Been there, done that.

Military junta. Now here's a form of government we could all get behind, if Colin Powell's bipartisan poll numbers are any measure. American citizens love a man in uniform—check out what cool threads did

for such wanky leaders as Grant and Ike, not to mention the popularity of *Evita*! With a junta, you get not one but several military strongmen! They promise to restore traditional values, scoff at bureaucracy, and do what needs to be done! And it eliminates the time and effort spent on voting! The only inconvenience: Junta dudes like to interrupt regularly scheduled TV programs.

As we've demonstrated above, good old-fashioned American republican democracy, with low voter turnout—don't forget that low voter turnout!—is still the preferred political system of choice here, especially for Gen-X/twentysomething/Baby-Buster types. Certainly republican democracy is easily corrupted by various powers that be, and nothing much ever gets done, but it does permit people to print zines and post Web sites and start bands with thirteen songs that are all about Abraham Lincoln. Democracy doesn't do anything *for* you, but its inefficiency is also its great advantage: It doesn't do anything *to* you, either.

16. THE PARTY'S OVER

*"Any man in his twenties who isn't a liberal has no heart.
Any man in his thirties who isn't a conservative has no brain."*
—*Dumb Disraeli quote*

n the United States being a good citizen means being active in politics. At least that's what my mom said. My involvement with the Democratic Party started at age nine, when she took me along to pass out McGovern-Shriver leaflets door-to-door in our solidly Republican neighborhood in Ohio. "The Democrats," my mother explained, "are the party of the people. Republicans only care about rich big shots."

Nothing I have seen since 1972 has contradicted the latter part of my mom's succinct summary of this nation's two-party system, with the amendment that the Democrats haven't been paying much attention to their populist past lately while the Republicans have remained scrupulously loyal to their history. Noting my mom's enthusiasm while she dialed number after number and tried to reason with our neighbors in a dingy campaign headquarters convinced me that there really was a chance of ousting President Nixon—a man who, all attempts at historical revisionism notwithstanding, was the devil incarnate.

My fourth-grade class held a mock election that fall. There were thirty-two little Nixonites to my one Democratic vote.

I quickly learned that, in America, Democrats usually lose, even when they win. Jimmy Carter squeaked by President Ford in 1976—an astonishing fact when you consider the unelected incumbent's corrupt pardon of Nixon and idiotic demeanor—and as a consequence never felt that he enjoyed a mandate to act like a real Democrat. Carter invented the New Democrat concept, a strategic rightward shift designed to appeal to conservative swing voters.

As a result, the great Reagan defense buildup actually began under Carter in 1978. He also initiated draft registration for males eighteen to twenty-six and refused to send U.S. athletes to attend the 1980 Moscow Olympics as retribution for the Soviet invasion of Afghanistan. Carter cost in 1980, mainly because swing voters abandoned him after the hostage crisis and these compromises had cost him his party's liberal base. Nonetheless, I volunteered for Mondale in '84 and Dukakis in '88, organizing college students and wheat-pasting posters in the subways, while Dems continued to pursue watered-down liberalism.

The capitalism-run-amok excesses of the Reagan and Bush years made it easier to be a Democrat again—by the time 1992 rolled around, even the most simpleminded voters couldn't be distracted from the recession by shadow issues like school prayer and flag burning. Nothing was more important to the country's political and financial health than getting George Herbert Hoover Walker Bush out of the White House. The day after the election, a reporter called to ask my reaction. "I feel like an evil cloud has lifted from the country," I told him as I labeled files at one of my three jobs. "Americans have rejected the idea that caring about other people is a sign of weakness."

Which brings me to my decision not to vote Democratic anymore.

While I am personally better off than I was in 1992, the country has continued to go to hell. The

reasons are simple. Given the first chance in a century to get national health-care legislation passed, Clinton blew it by proposing an outlandish managed-care scheme designed to protect insurance-company profits. Then he pushed for and signed NAFTA and GATT, treasonous free-trade deals that sold out American workers to improve his corporate pals' bottom lines.

Even Reagan and Bush never expended their political capital on free trade. To be sure, Clinton did the right thing by sending troops to Bosnia, but he waited so long that the people they were sent to protect were all dead by the time our soldiers got there.

Clinton's 1995 copresidency with Newt Gingrich was a strange stylistic embarrassment, but the last straw for me was his cynical election-year betrayal of the poor: a welfare-reform bill that eliminated much of the welfare system without providing any safety net—or even poorly paid jobs—to replace it.

My friends argue that voting for a third party—or for that matter, opting to stay home and watch TV—is a de facto vote for the Republicans. In a rigid two-party system, they're statistically correct, but so what? In the 1996 election, Dole and Clinton were both essentially the same: pro-business, pro-choice, and deficit-obsessed. A Dole administration might have cost the nation a few progressive appellate judges, but on the issues that really matter, most Americans wouldn't have noticed much difference.

Voting Democratic tells the party that you agree with everything they've done so far when you're in fact merely voting for the anti-Republicans. If you support NAFTA and guaranteed unemployment and making children homeless, fine. But our repub-

DEMOCRATS AND REPUBLICANS
The Differences at a Glance

ISSUE	DEMOCRATS	REPUBLICANS
Abortion Rights	Democrats are pro-choice, except that in the South they don't talk about it.	Republicans are pro-life, except that in the North they never mention it.
Creating Jobs	Democrats believe that job creation is a top priority unless it interferes with bond prices.	Job creation is OK whenever first approved by investment bankers.
Defense Budget	Democrats support expensive arms buildup but try to appear as wimpy as possible.	Republicans support expensive arms buildup.
Flag Burning Amendment	Democrats do not actively encourage the desecration of the American flag.	Republicans actively discourage burning the flag.
Free Trade Agreements	Democrats favor all free-trade agreements because they encourage a higher standard of living for overseas workers.	Republicans favor all free-trade agreements because they encourage a higher standard of living for American stockholders.
Human Rights Overseas	Democrats see human rights as an important priority in foreign relations, but don't press the issue when business is involved.	Republicans, who back big-business interests overseas, don't care about human rights because they interfere with profits.
Immigration Policy	Democrats see America as a nation made rich by its diversity, yet oppose opening the borders to legal immigrants.	Republicans see America as a nation made rich by the diversity of Northern European immigrants during the previous two centuries.
School Prayer	Democrats oppose school prayer on the grounds of constitutional separation of church and state.	Republicans, while favoring theoretical school prayer, oppose actual school prayer on the grounds of poor public opinion ratings.
The War on Drugs	Democrats support filling American jails with crack smokers.	Republicans support filling American jails with pot smokers.
Welfare Reform	Democrats reluctantly approve of eventually throwing all welfare recipients out into the streets.	Republicans enthusiastically support eventually throwing all welfare recipients out into the streets.

lic wasn't intended to have voters support the lesser of two evils, or likely winners simply because they're likely to win. If you substantially disagree with Democrats who act like Republicans, you have a moral obligation as a citizen to vote for someone else. If no other candidate appeals to you, your duty is to stay home.

Some people may question how I could abandon the Democrats after all this time.

Traditional, reasonable Republicans know that minimizing government regulation is in conflict with their anti-abortion positions. But like the Democrats, the GOP has shifted right in search of the would-be Nazis among us. The thing is, fascists don't make up a big voting bloc in this country, so why cater to them?

Neither the Democrats nor the Republicans care about changing the world—they just

But I never left the party; it left me, and I suspect that a lot of Republicans—the ones who support fiscal moderation, minimal government interference, and low taxes—feel the same way I do about "their" party.

The sickening display of right-wing Christian fundamentalism at the last few Republican National Conventions was a microcosm of the takeover of the GOP on the local level by racists, homophobes, and morons of every other imaginable variety.

want to win, no matter what the cost, which leads to mad ideological floundering in search of the perfect formula for success.

Anyone who doubts that something a tad inconsistent is taking place in the Party of the Twice-Married White Male has only to refer to Bob Dole's attacks on heartless corporate downsizing in the '96 race. The GOP isn't really drifting left—it's lurching all over the ideological spectrum like a desperate ad agency scrambling for the ideal jingle.

The GOP's roots in an ideological past became evident in Dole's attempts to stir up resentment against "liberal Bill Clinton" and his "liberal agenda." Insults that worked against George McGovern don't fly anymore because voters realize that Clinton is no more liberal than the Mets or the Bengals.

And that's the point: Voters have become sports fans—they flock to candidates with good packaging, and everybody loves a win-

really matter, but that's been going on since the first time a candidate applied pancake makeup to go on TV. More important, it renders election results meaningless, inasmuch as voter-fans can't register their positions on issues when none of the candidates on the ballot take stands on any issues.

Imagery decides elections now, not issues, so election data mean zip. As the essential symbiosis between government and

ner. The result is a syllogism Ionesco would love: Third-party candidate Ross Perot's polls were low; therefore, people didn't vote for him; ergo, he lost. Q.E.D.

Americans disliked Clinton personally and didn't expect him to improve their lives, but they voted for him in droves anyway—after all, as the projected winner, his reelection was inevitable.

The death of party ideology has meant an end to serious discussion of issues that

popular opinion rots away over time, citizens will become increasingly alienated from their leaders, and their leaders won't have a clue where to lead them.

For now, the big problem for an amoral, rudderless president like Clinton and his party of hyperkinetic fanboys is their inability to cope with the future.

Not long ago, it was possible for any American to predict how strongly defined ideologues like LBJ and Reagan might react

to almost anything. Guys like Clinton have platforms to guide them on existing issues like gun control and abortion, but they have to analyze opinion polls before they can take a position on anything new and unexpected. In '96 Bob Dole even went so far as to publicly disclaim his party's platform, proudly announcing that he hadn't even read the thing.

It's tempting to say that the triumph of ersatz politics isn't the end of the world. As the millions of Americans who spend their weekends cheering for teams conceived in NFL marketing meetings can attest, it can be a lot of fun. It's also the kind of thing that brings down governments and leads to economic and social collapse. We're a consumerist society, after all, and political platforms are to candidates what labels are to products. When I buy a Coke, there had better be Coke—not Diet Coke, not Pepsi—in that can, dammit. You're entitled to know what you're getting when you buy a carbonated beverage. You ought to be able to know what you're getting when you hand over the launch codes and the future of the country as well.

17. CHOOSING MY RELIGION

"You will be assimilated. Resistance is futile."
—*The Borg*, Star Trek: The Next Generation

My friend Debra was born into a Roman Catholic family. She got baptized and confirmed and everything; sometimes she even confessed. But twenty years of reciting the same old liturgies gets pretty tiresome, no matter how much you believe in God. By the time she turned thirty-five, she only went to Mass when her parents came to town.

People are afraid to die. No, people are *fucking terrified out of their goddamn minds* that they're going to die. Nobody knows what, if anything, comes after we flat-line, but we suspect that a big black nothing is a hell of a lot more likely than spending eternity sitting on an oversize lotus blossom or hanging out in the clouds with winged guys playing harps. But we need to delude ourselves into such fanciful visions of an afterlife; otherwise we'll all go mad.

Debra, like everyone else, was determined to find a faith so that she could set aside her fear of mortality and concentrate on more important concerns, like dating and picking the right 401(k). She had given up on politics long ago, gotten tired of punk rock, and become so jaded by the impossibility of love in a technologically advanced society that she'd sworn off sex. Moreover, as time passed, Debra began to fear that her life had lost its meaning. She felt empty, unfocused, aimless. So, one crisp afternoon in the fall, she decided to go shopping for a new religion.

"I can buy any car I want. Why can't I choose my faith the same way? There are so many religions out there that my parents never even considered. Who's to say the pope's guys have a monopoly on meaning?"

I was intrigued by Debra's consumerist approach to finding a higher truth. It was very American. An erratic Catholic myself, I suddenly began to think: "Maybe, despite all evidence to the contrary, God really *does* exist. Perhaps I've just been using the wrong long-distance service provider!"

I decided to tag along with Debra and check out what the other faiths had to say.

PROTESTANTISM

A week later, I agreed to meet Debra after work at an impressive Methodist cathedral on New York's Fifth Avenue. I got there first, in the middle of a torrential downpour. As I waited outside, I read the *Post* and checked out the architecture, which was both an homage to and an obvious rip-off of Westminster Abbey. Prestigious address, though, and within walking distance of work.

Debra arrived. As we entered the church, an ominous sixtysomething minister urged his tiny flock: "Acknowledge your wretchedness!" He went on and on after that, but you know what they say about first impressions. Afterward, at the 84th Street multiplex, Debra interrogated me. "So, whadja think?"

"My boss reminds me how wretched I am all day long," I said. "I spend most of my waking hours trying to forget my wretchedness, not acknowledge it."

"Yeah, I know what you mean," Debra said ruefully.

JUDAISM

Next Debra asked a Jewish friend, Paul, to escort us to Yom Kippur services at a synagogue on the Upper West Side. Famous for its outspoken left-wing rabbi, this Reform temple appealed to our political sensibilities, as well as being convenient to a number of excellent Chinese restaurants.

The day before, Paul called Debra to remind us to buy tickets to the service. "Tickets? What for?" Debra asked. Paul explained that Yom Kippur was an important day of worship, and that, as at any desirable event, seats commanded a high price. It was sort of like a Rolling Stones concert. Accordingly, tickets were $50 each.

Although Debra had the fifty bucks, her upbringing had led her to believe that religion should be free, except when one is guilted into dropping money into a collection plate. We promised to buy Stones tickets the next time they were in town.

ISLAM

A few nights later, Debra and I were studying the Cliff Notes to the Koran over double cappuccinos at Starbucks. "Islam is pretty cool," she said, turning the pages. "Listen to this: 'Hell awaits the infidels.'" I agreed that any religion that permitted you to use the word "infidel" in ordinary conversation was worth looking into.

We took the subway uptown to the recently constructed postmodern mosque on East 96th Street. The gate was closed.

Hours weren't posted.

"How the hell did they get to be America's fastest-growing religion without being open?" Debra sneered.

"You don't need a mosque, you know," I said helpfully. "Wherever you are, you just pray five times a day facing Mecca."

It was just as well. Debra would never have been able to afford the imported prayer rugs we'd admired down in SoHo.

BUDDHISM

Later that night, Debra and I gulped down half-price margaritas with Tanya, a thirty-year-old ex–Southern Baptist from Oregon. She'd become a Buddhist after seeing *The Last Emperor.*

Tanya tugged on a diamond earring. "My cat is like a little Bodhisattva. He watches you to find out what object you love the most. Then he breaks it to reduce your ties to earthly material possessions. If you fail the test by yielding to frustration, you may not make it to the next level, much less the magnificent void of Nirvana."

"Eastern religions are too difficult," Debra whispered to me. "I could never remember all those weird vocabulary words." I empathized. Buddhists are much smarter than I am. We decided to leave Buddhism to the movies.

CHRISTIAN SCIENCE

The next day, Debra called me, completely out of breath. "I met a Christian Scientist on the subway today," she said. "She told me that I can start saving all the money I spend on health insurance! All I have to do is pray!"

"What if you get hit by a bus?" I asked. "Would you be able, as a Christian Scientist, to go to the hospital?"

"Well, I'd just pray really, really hard," she said, trying to be optimistic.

"Yeah, but what if the front tire had gone over your torso, and your organs were squished everywhere and your lungs had exploded and half of your blood was in the sewer and both of your arms were broken so you couldn't pray? What then?"

Neither of us said anything for what seemed like a very long time.

"Sounds pretty dumb," she said, finally.

CATHOLICISM

I didn't hear from Debra for a few weeks. She was too busy sorting through solicitation letters she'd received from the Episcopalians, Presbyterians, Jehovah's Witnesses, and Mormons. She even downloaded a tract on Taoism from the Web.

Then she called me at work. "I've decided to become a Catholic!" she told me. "It's familiar, I already know the prayers, and the Masses are only forty-five minutes long."

Debra had her second confirmation, at a predominantly gay parish in the West Village, in early December. The church was a modest post-Federalist building, but it was directly across the street from an express subway station, and the Waverly Diner was just a block away. It was a beautiful ceremony, and Debra looked radiant in her puffy white dress. "I think it's great that you've finally found what you've been looking for, and just in time for Christmas," I told her supportively.

Debra looked at me scornfully. "You're not off the hook yet. Next week we're checking out the Hindus."

Business as Usual— The Sequel

SAN FRANCISCO (Rutters)—Sharon Walsh doesn't have to ask her sixteen-year-old son Brad where he's been. She knows he was shooting pool from 3:45 to 4:53, trying to scam beer at the 7-Eleven from 5:02 to 5:07, and halfway home, screaming insults at pedestrians from his friend's car at 5:33. "I don't know how I'd parent without this information," Ms. Walsh says.

Brad's movements are monitored by a tiny microchip that tracks a person's every movement, a device developed by a Silicon Valley company Tekgeex, a subsidiary of Conglomco of Mountain View, California, has already implanted the chips in more than ten thousand people.

"We started with microchips that track and identify animals. This was the next logical step," said Justine Nowicki, CEO of Tekgeex. Tekgeex stock closed at 140 on the NYSE on December 31, up 32 points from the previous quarter.

The chips are planted just under the right shoulder blade and are so tiny that a sleeping trackee can be injected without being awoken, as in Brad's case. (Technically, Brad was drugged at the time.) Each microchip is encoded with the person's name, address, Social Security number, magazine subscription data, permanent record from elementary school, purchases made with ATM cards, and other information. Satellites can pinpoint an implant's precise location as far as two hundred meters below the earth's surface, where many people live.

Unruly teens are only the beginning. AT&T, IBM, and other Fortune 500 companies are ordering the implants for their employees in order to increase their productivity. Bill Gates, chairman of Microsoft, mused aloud: "When I pay my employees, their time belongs to me. Why should I pay them to make personal phone calls or go to the bathroom? Now I don't have to."

Please see editorial, "On the Right Track," page 312.

18. MY DAUGHTER IS A TEEN LESBIAN LAP DANCER!

"Your stuff is shit. My shit is stuff."
—*George Carlin, 1972*

They've torched Huck Finn. They've censored the Internet. All the great institutions that once held this country together—family, religion, patriotism—have crumbled away, but through it all one bastion of hope remained: television. Then they forced the networks to rate their programs using a system no one understands. Now the Christian fundamentalists who run America have turned on tabloid TV talk shows.

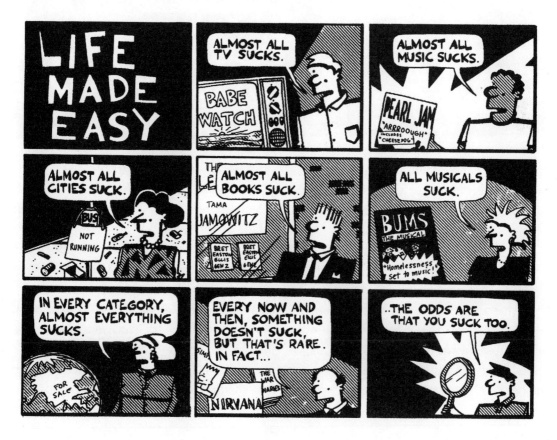

At first glance, daytime "trash television" looks like a big fat target for censorship. Such wholesome broadcasts as Jenny Jones's "Punk Rock Makeover," Ricki Lake's "I Do Drugs with My Kids," and Jerry Springer's "Poor Black Teen Buries Her Baby Alive" are exploitative themes in the finest tradition of the American kitsch aesthetic. It might seem obvious that these shows are crap, pure and simple—a waste of valuable airtime—and should be done away with, the sooner the better. Not to worry, Pat Robertson and his not-so-merry crew are on the case!

Even a liberal pundit like columnist Bob Herbert of *The New York Times* compares talk-show hosts and their producers to "pornographers and pimps." CBS-TV *60 Minutes* correspondent Mike Wallace, no Christian Coalition member himself, bashes tabloid journalism and says he blames talk shows such as *The Jenny Jones Show, Ricki Lake,* and *Sally* for the "cheap exploitation of people who shouldn't have agreed to appear in the first place."

The problem is, Ricki Lake cares more about the country than do Bill Clinton, Dan Rather, or Ralph Reed.

After having watched hundreds of hours of these programs, I have found that they address more of the real, day-to-day problems of ordinary Americans than all other broadcast and print media combined. At no time is this more obvious than in an era in which political candidates try to fire up crowds by calling for a 2 percent reduction in interest rates and controversies rage over how to calculate the cost-of-living index.

Teenage pregnancy, suicide, joblessness, shattered marriages, custody battles, incest, AIDS, and the despair of depressed people who don't know why they bother to get up in the morning is the essence of daytime talk. It's also the stuff of most American lives. Viewers are responsive because they see people like themselves discussing issues that matter to them, no matter how lurid or downscale they may seem to consumers of *The Atlantic Monthly* or *The NewsHour with Jim Lehrer.*

Naturally, most of the politicians and columnists who lambaste these shows obviously never watch them. I, as someone who works all day at home, do. So please allow me to help you Princeton grads out. Here are some important points for snobs who want the lowdown on daytime talk and the current state of America without having to invest time you'd otherwise spend watching Merchant/Ivory films:

Talk-show guests are average Americans. George Will need not apply here. The American mass media have been usurped by the cult of the professional expert, but not in the world of daytime talk. Denizens of trailer parks and ghettos, the products of broken homes and lousy educations, people the elite call the scum of the earth—they're all here, shouting at each other, crying, spewing invective and malapropisms, in all of their loud, tacky glory. They are the great neglected majority—and they vote.

Not all talk shows are alike. Many suffer from dimwitted hosts and trite topics. If I have to sit through another *Jenny Jones* "My Daughter Dresses Like a Punk; Please Give Her a Makeover" show again, I'll do a triple back flip off the George Washington Bridge. Others, like *The Oprah Winfrey Show* and *The Maury Povitch Show,* have become as stale and out-of-touch as Congress. But the best talk shows offer entertainment and insight, such as Richard Bey's erstwhile gutter-level, semi–game show format and Ricki Lake's fast-paced, multimedia Gen X style, as well as incisive coverage of long-neglected topics.

Trash TV is educational. If you've ever wondered how racists think or why teenagers get pregnant, put down *The New Yorker* and tune in. For example, I watched a mother who disapproved of her daughter's interra-

cial marriage call herself "purebred" because she was herself "a quarter blue-blood Russian, a quarter blue-blood Hungarian, a quarter blue-blood American Indian, and a quarter blue-blood Irish." She considers herself "blue-blood, pure." This woman's surreal eugenics may not be pleasant to listen to, but her reasoning is not at all uncommon. You need to know about her and people like her. Why? Because there are a lot of these simpletons out there—and they vote.

Trash TV is therapeutic. Unlike mainstream televised forums like *60 Minutes,* many talk-show hosts actually attempt to resolve the problems they discuss right then and there on the air. The 1995 murder of a gay man by a straight guy confronted with his "secret admirer" on the *The Jenny Jones Show* is often cited as an example of irresponsible television, but the only person to blame was the dirtbag who pulled the trigger. Anyway, that was a freak event. Even

Richard Bey used to spring for shrinks; Montel Williams offered his production team to help design more effective antidrug advertisements.

Montel Williams Is God. If you watch no other talk show, watch *The Montel Williams Show.* About half of this brilliant man's shows are based on "serious" topics, such as how to fight drugs and gang violence and improve secondary education. Although the former marine hosts his share of shoutfests, he is always interested in solving the problems he discusses. I once attended a *Montel* taping on school violence. Interestingly, the most worthless, out-of-touch comments were spewed from the lips of the "experts" on the panel, Assistant Secretary of Education Madelaine Kunen and a syndicated columnist. The secretary's solution to school violence—"When someone hits you, talk to them instead of hitting them back"—reminded

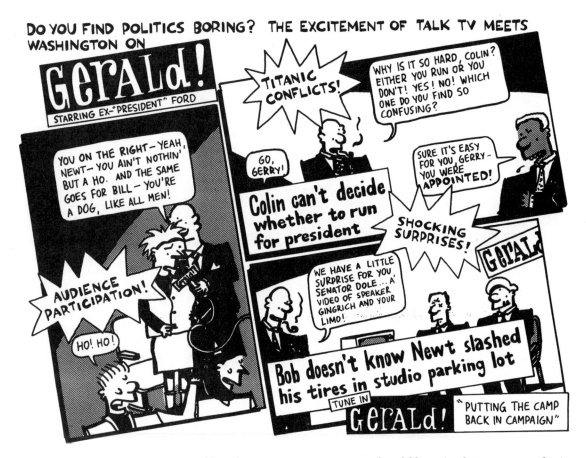

me that our country is governed by idiots.

By contrast, a "white trash" seventh-grader (coincidentally from the same town in Ohio where I grew up) who'd been beaten on the bus by twelve-year-old thugs offered real insight into structural dynamics: "The administrators just don't care. They're not paid to care."

If the Bible-thumpers and the white-wine-and-brie set have their way, the only discussion we'll have as a society will concern the whether the Federal Reserve dis-

count rate should be raised. But many television viewers, whether they're black, female, young, or poor, are tired of being told to shut up. The talk shows provide the great masses of ordinary Americans—people who are otherwise excluded from our national dialogue—an opportunity for real input. Isn't it better to scream at one another in a TV studio than to toss bricks in the streets?

These would-be censors are lurid and dangerously stupid. Hell, *they* should be banned.

19. LIKE, I PIERCED MY NIPPLE BRANDS WITH A NAIL

*"If you don't remember the 1968 Chicago Democratic Convention,
the Summer of Love, Kent State, you missed everything."*
—*My ninth-grade English teacher*

At first glance, my friend's boyfriend looks just like everybody else, when everybody else is a twenty-seven-year-old guy: goatee, short bowl cut, Miller Beer jacket, and, according to my friend, assorted piercings. Since I've never seen him in the buff, I had to ask: "Where are the piercings?" "All the usual places," my friend replied, "including his penis."

As a guy myself, and being the kind of guy who was very poorly brought up, I decided to turn the inquiry on its subject. "So, Doug," I ventured casually over a micro-brewed beer that tasted like brake fluid, "how does that pierce work? Does it go through the, uh, well, you know, the urethra?"

He allowed that it did.

"Didn't it hurt?"

"Well, sure, but it seemed like the thing to do at the time," he replied. "The only thing is, I have to sit down when I take a leak. Otherwise it'll spray all over my legs."

So much for the primary advantage of being male.

Formerly the domain of discount prostitutes, street gangs, bikers, and bondage clubs, even the most extreme forms of self-mutilation have become popular among yupper-middle-class mall rats and low-level executives. The most common question I've gotten at parties lately has been what kind of

tattoo do I have and where. The possibility that I might not have gotten one at all yet is too absurd to contemplate. After all, no one questions whether or not you have an e-mail address, right?

Now no self-respecting woman allows herself to be seen outside without her set of matching (and connected) eyelid and navel rings. Similarly, polite society has to question the masculinity, not to mention the patriotism, of any male unwilling to run a lattice of tiny ink-filled needles through his skin in homage to his favorite golfer or trip-hop band.

The cutting edge of Gen X fashion is decidedly masochistic. Anyone can look good without going to too much effort, but it's a real challenge to use clothing and body hair to intentionally make yourself look worse than you otherwise would. Shrinks say we're all just trying to get back at our parents for abandoning us, but it's actually a full-blown rebellion against Baby Boom aesthet-

ics. Let Jane Fonda flaunt her washboard stomach and buns of steel at age fifty-nine and Mick Jagger bounce around the stage while belting out "Under My Thumb" at age fifty-four; we're gonna work on *our* stomachs with Miller and cattle brands.

Speaking of which, after a brief surge of interest in March 1996, branding appears to have fallen out of favor among young adults. "I had a big Circle A for anarchy branded on my back," an old libertarian classmate of mine confided. "But the scar tissue falls off, and you can barely see it now. I bet it'll be gone within a year or two."

"Did it hurt?" I wanted to know.

"Of *course* it hurt! Do you think I liked spending a hundred twenty-five dollars on a scar that won't see the end of the decade?"

Contemporary youth culture is at a crossroads, stymied between two equally unappealing choices: reverting to the staid old fashions of the Gap and the Salvation Army, or stagnating at the triple ear-pierce and standard-issue thorn tattoo around the upper arm. Now that tattoos are as common as ATM cards and leather zipper masks are acceptable evening wear, where else can a fashion victim turn to stand out in the crowd?

To ever more extremes, that's where.

Practically everyone from Keanu Reeves to Alan Greenspan has a pierced tongue, but when's the last time you saw someone with a railroad spike drilled into his skull?

Surgical studs—tacks attached to your bones through your skin—are still somewhat unusual, but risking tetanus every time you take a shower gets old fast. Having both arms and legs removed makes a far

BACK TO SCHOOL

GOODBYE 1970s...
EIGHTIES RETRO IS HERE!

CHOOSING YOUR MAJOR
Find an area of study compatible with your race, gender and religion!

MADONNA REDUX:
Wearing Your Underwear *Underneath*

COOL POWER TIE!

MY DAD TOOK IT OFF A DEAD COMMODITIES TRADER BACK IN '87!

Making fun of the fat kid: An American Classic!

BASEBALL CAPS: FASHION FAUX PAS?	CONDOMS, CONDOMS, CONDOMS! They're fun. They're easy-to-use. They're free!	FOILING YOUR SCHOOL'S METAL DETECTOR

more compelling statement about the impotence of humanity in a post-technological world—and allows you to lose forty to eighty pounds without dieting. Moreover, you can always tie your severed limbs to a chain attached to your belt loops. Talk about making a splash at the next tailgate party!

For those with a vivid imagination and a strong affinity for pain, self-mutilation offers unlimited possibilities for making a striking accessorizing statement. Are you into goth music? Create your own stigmata by pounding sharp glass tubes into your hands and feet! Dance-floor denizens can inject cesium into their bloodstreams: They'll glow when the strobe lights go off!

New advances in surgical reconstruction allow you to rearrange your body parts. You'll look just like the FTD man—and you'll be able to hear ants—when you have your ears moved to your ankles!

The natural process of aging also presents new opportunities for the innovative stylist. Around age thirty you'll start develop-

ing nose and ear hairs. But don't trim those unsightly hormonal protrusions—braid them together for a whole new look that says: "I'm old and I'm bold!" Similarly, old tattoos will bleed into a morass of blue dye. You can make the best of a bad situation by having your entire body dyed that same exact shade of blue. Bald spots, paunches, and sags all open up brand-new palettes for tattooing.

As for me, I've been holding out during the Great American Mutilation Renaissance.

What fun is there in getting the same old nose bone or cellular telephone arm implant that my accountant has? It took a long time, and a lot of thought, but I've finally decided upon the ultimate nihilistic statement, the one that really says *me*: I'm planning to have twenty-foot-long leather wings surgically attached to my torso so I can soar high above Central Park, cackling madly at the people below. My neighbor Stan already had his done, and they look great.

20. THE SPORTING LIFE

"3 million Americans depleted a total of $686 million to spend an average of 22 days of the 1996 calendar year hunting migratory birds."
—*Statistical Abstract of the United States*

I wasn't bothering anyone. I had the right to be left alone. There I was, taking my legally mandated fifteen-minute break—a sacred right that thousands of soldiers died fighting Nazi Germany to protect—in the twenty-third-floor men's room of the bank where I worked. I was washing my hands, as all good Americans do after you-know-what, when Miguel came in and asked The Question.

"So, Ted," he said with a smirk, "how about that game last night?"

My mind raced—was this football or baseball season? Do they play basketball in May? Were any New York teams doing unusually well? If so, who would be the opponent? Are we talking pro or college sports? Most important, did New York win? A truthful answer—spectator sports are to a productive society what mildew is to a men's room—would have impugned my already-dubious masculinity. So I lied.

"Yeah, some game! It-was-really-exciting."

"Did you go or watch it on TV?" Miguel wanted to know. I couldn't imagine why he cared about how I spent my spare time. Clearly he was planning to file a memo with the personnel department, with a cc to various government agencies, after this interrogation. The backs of my knees began perspiring.

"Um, on TV," I said, just to be safe. Of the seventy channels I get on cable, sixty-

three of them are devoted to shots of people hitting, throwing, carrying, and chasing balls. As far as I can tell, every activity vaguely related to sports, including backyard Frisbee in Wisconsin and professional golf, is broadcast nationally (usually when *60 Minutes* is scheduled to air) and then later discussed at length in daily papers and monthly magazines with an enthusiasm otherwise reserved for analysis of the Camper van Beethoven reunion tour.

"Gotcha!" Miguel scoffed. "The game wasn't on TV! It was called due to rain! I shall immediately notify everyone via company e-mail that you are homosexual."

I attempted to salvage the situation as Miguel dashed into the hall: "Fine! Go ahead! I'll tell everyone we were in the rest room together! That makes *you* gay too!"

It was too late. Several months afterward, I yielded to social pressure and married a man I met at a hardware store. Another

heterosexual bites the dust, all due to the American sports fetish.

More and more male Americans—with the exception of lesbians, women are permitted to hate sports—are clashing with a social norm that expects them to spend their weekends glued to their televisions to watch the high drama of guys driving cars in circles and bouncing balls on a wood floor. Tragically, most guys under thirty-five were raised by single or divorced mothers. Fathers, who are traditionally responsible for indoctrina-

tion into sports culture, all left the country to enforce free-trade agreements. The result is that two whole generations of guys spent their youths unpacking boxes at the UPS plant to help pay for supper instead of beating up their friends to get at a ball. Most destructive to the intergenerational propagation of sports, however, is perpetual bad-mouthing from the harbingers of maternalism: "Thank God your father abandoned you and left me to starve. Otherwise, he'd just be sitting there on the couch drinking

beer and screaming at the Knicks, using racist epithets."

Generational politics have also diminished the impact of competitive athletics on Gen Xers. No one in their right mind would ever consider mixing it up on the football field after getting their nipples pierced with little hoops. The group dynamics of sports—the Wave, the Nuremberg Rally–like atmosphere of a typical stadium, the beer bellies quavering over Harley-Davidson belt buckles—all conflict with the post-punk aesthetics of young American males, whose role models lean more toward Richard Hell than Magic Johnson. The patron saint of Xdom, Kurt Cobain, hated jocks and often asked them to leave his concerts. So it's no accident that the latest icon of professional sports, Tiger Woods, is a slight, awkward guy who plays golf, the least sportlike of sports. Even so, he dresses like a serious geek, which leaves pseudo-punk Dennis Rodman the Xer sports crown. After all, he got his nose pierced on MTV!

As today's young adults age, it's likely that sports will start to recede in importance as a form of entertainment, and that memorizing batting averages will not forever remain an indicator of masculinity. Most spectator sports are, after all, slow-moving and dull, and the national attention span has been noticeably shortened in recent years. Post-Reagan America is fiercely individualistic, rendering the team concept obsolete. And the family continues to evaporate, with fathers becoming collateral damage.

Until then, of course, the young and childless will have to defend their alienated and disaffected personalities through a world of homophobic Miguels. I recommend the following survival strategies:

Raise the jargon ante. That's right—invent sports jargon that doesn't exist in order to confuse the Miguel in question. "I couldn't believe the QVAs on that second base line! I would have given anything to see the look on the backup coach when he delineated that passing strat!" This has never failed to work for me, even

to the point of causing the victim to doubt his *own* masculinity.

Fight fire with fire. Defuse the situation by wallowing in confession. "Yes, it's true—I'm gay! I have sex with other men! Last night, while the Game was on, I was rolling under the sheets in a leather zipper mask with a state assemblyman!" Typically the Miguel will move on, just to get away from you.

Pull out your gun and shoot the guy. Not recommended unless the aforementioned techniques fail, but the Second Amendment should always be properly exploited.

Granted, you could always start reading the sports section, and going to some games, and learning about sports. You might even consider hanging out in a sports bar—believe it or not, there are drinking establishments strictly devoted to sports fans—although you would be in dire risk of having to engage in sports-related conversation. But what's the point? Take it from me: The love of another man isn't that bad—unless he's a sports fan.

21. WHO NEEDS THE NEWS?

> "Let's say I hire you. Can you guarantee me that I'll never see people out in the parking lot protesting something you've drawn?"
>
> —*Editor considering me for a position as staff cartoonist*

For the past hundred years, Americans have found their news in the daily paper. The rise of radio, and then television, did nothing to stop that simple fact: Network news programs may have more viewers than newspapers have readers, but they're only watched because of their immediacy. As a nation we've always viewed nonprint news as a supplement to the more serious, indepth coverage of the daily paper. Now, however, the average newspaper reader is pushing fifty. And new readership is so flat that the average newspaper reader may be dead in thirty years.

The big-city daily, the grand institution of the American 20th century, seems about to go the way of the era itself, but no one's paying much attention. A typical casualty was the *Phoenix Gazette*, an afternoon paper that, after 116 years, printed its last issue in early 1997, its demise apparently caused by an old ailment: Americans prefer their written news in the morning. After toiling all day for Disney, Microsoft, Nike, or whoever owns what's left of the country these days, Americans seemingly can't absorb informa-

tion any heavier than televised info nibblets. This trend extends even to San Francisco, where the objectively superior *Examiner* is inexplicably gasping for breath in its long battle with the clunky, 1950s-style *Chronicle*.

Even the surviving morning papers are suffering. Victimized by incompetent management, intransigent unions, unpredictable spikes in newsprint prices, and the decline of big-ticket advertisers (such as department stores), even leviathans like the *Los Angeles Times* have been forced to reduce costs. In

New York, a city of voracious readers who just a few decades ago took twenty-six daily papers to work with them on the subway, the well-written but pitifully designed *New York Newsday* discovered that it couldn't compete successfully with the *News, Post,* and *Times*—of which only the last could be reasonably called financially stable.

It doesn't take a professional demographer to see that unless the average age of newspaper readers stops increasing as quickly as the passage of time, newspapers will soon be joining the history they'd rather be recording. The American Society of Newspaper Editors, however, needed a poll to tell them that 40 million Generation Xers (Americans in their later twenties and early thirties) don't read the daily paper. This cluelessness is partially indicative of how the industry got into this mess in the first place.

Editors know that their younger would-be readers are turning instead to free-distribution alternative weeklies and the bottomless pit of information available on the Internet

for their media fix. Where their elders used TV news as a supplement to the newspaper, for them TV often *is* the news.

I see the trend among my own peers, most of whom are college-educated and have plenty of disposable income. They pick up the paper on Mondays for the sports statistics, on Fridays for the movie listings, or on Sundays for the classifieds. With the exception of those who make their livings by commenting on current events, I don't know anyone who reads a daily every day. Every-

one reads a weekly or two, and perhaps a news-oriented Web site like HotWired.

Besides price, the primary appeal of the weeklies is youth-based content. While typically devoid of breaking news—an obvious shortcoming of a weekly deadline—alternative weeklies offer non-news features that people under forty can actually use. The typical daily, meanwhile, doesn't look much different than it did a half-century ago. Many still have a society page!

Many younger Americans feel guilty for

not reading the paper. "I know I should, but I don't," goes the refrain, but why should they? Where I live in New York, none of the three dailies offers coverage of new albums, concerts, or books that would interest anyone under fifty. The *Times* commonly refers to restaurants that cost $50 per person as "intermediate" and discusses opera, dance, and musical theater as if those forms weren't as dead as Cole Porter; the *News* considers Garth Brooks the cutting edge of popular music; and the *Post* hasn't even heard of the Internet. So my peers turn to *The Village Voice* and *NYPress*, the two dominant free weeklies that appear on Wednesdays and offer extensive housing and concert listings. The trouble is: What do you read the rest of the week?

The death of the dailies is a slow-motion national crisis. Association of Alternative Newsweeklies president Jeff vonKaenel wrote in the trade journal *Editor & Publisher* that "the idea of having no more dailies scares me," but at this point the dailies are nothing more than a foil for the more informative and relevant free weeklies. Even with their modestly increasing circulations, local weeklies will never possess sufficient capital to hire scores of journalists and photographers to cover the planet and question the barrage of propaganda pumped out by government and big business; on the other hand, that poverty keeps them relatively free of corporate and government influence. Gen Xers aren't stupid for finding endless economic analyses, foreign policy editorials, and campaign platforms boring—these products of the Baby Boomer White House have nothing to do with them anyway. Readers under forty care a lot more about their next trip to Baja California than Al Gore's latest bureaucratic-streamlining plan.

The Internet isn't the answer either. Few public spaces are wired with decent online equipment. A decent PC costs $3,500, plus $240 a year for a typical service provider. For the foreseeable future, the information turnpike will be open only to the nation's richest 20 percent. Nothing is, or will be, as cheap, portable, or comprehensive as the daily paper—or even as widely read. A country without a common source of information and arbiter of issues is on a sure path to balkanization and tribalism, and that's exactly what we're getting. While TV news is widely disseminated, the increasing number of cable news channels and all-news networks only further individualizes the American experience—and thoughtful consideration of the issues is intrinsically opposed to television's primary imperative: entertainment.

Ironically, the vast resources available to big dailies from their media-conglomerate parent companies is also their strength. Their only hope for survival lies in rebuilding circulation by recapturing their former roles

as advocates of democracy with populist, anticorporate investigative reporting. Weeklies should do what they do best—act as radical watchdogs of the mainstream media and offer edgy features that others are too afraid to print.

Perhaps the simultaneous rise of media conglomerates and the decline of independent journalism is coincidental, but it's certain that that corporate owners have little interest in encouraging newspapers and other information outlets to challenge those in power. The less Americans know what's going on, the better things are for the executive class. Given how far the pendulum has swung in favor of the business establishment, this is a frightening phenomenon.

The corporate influence on journalism is best exemplified by market segmenting. While older magazines like *Time* and *Newsweek* attempt to draw in a mass market, newer publications cater to incredibly minute market segments, like white Midwestern males aged sixteen to nineteen.

If current trends continue, everyone will read their own magazine, devoted exclusively to themselves—in fact, that's how the Internet versions of daily newspapers see their future. Every morning over food supplement 104-A and ersatz coffee I'll download my copy of *Ted—The Zine,* which will contain all sorts of exciting articles about Vichy France, Billy Childish, and my cat, Indy. True, I won't learn anything that I don't already know in the first place, but that's life. Happenstance will become a thing of the past, until eventually no one will know anything because they had no previous knowledge to expand upon.

Because no one will read the same news, watch the same films, or share a common identity, no one will have anything to say to anyone else. We'll all be alone in a crowd, vulnerable to whatever lies and nonsense our leaders choose to shove down our throats. Fortunately, we'll never notice the difference.

22. http://www.timewaster. com/~slack/nada

"The system is not available. Please try again in 46 minutes."
—*AOL error message*

"They relied on the Internet in case of nuclear war, right?"
—*Graffiti in cybercafé rest room, Philadelphia*

When I was in college, I became hopelessly infatuated with a girl who cheated on me, forgot my birthday, and wasn't even that pretty. My friends referred to her physique as "Frank Purdue's Mix 'n' Match Parts" because she was petite above the waist and pearlike below. She wasn't terribly bright or well read. She voted for Reagan. She thought the peak of American musical accomplishment occurred at the release of the Scorpions' second LP. But our sexual chemistry was so strong that I couldn't live without her. I was pretty stupid.

My love-hate relationship with the Internet is a lot like that. The thing is massively overhyped, and it certainly isn't about to create a sense of community among Americans, or among the citizens of the world. If anything, it's keeping us out of the bars and cafés and Laundromats where we might actually talk to one another and tying us up at home, sitting on our collective asses waiting for our modems to connect. It's slow, frustrating, and incredibly disappointing. Even the alt.sex Usenet groups aren't sexy. But I can't imagine life without it.

I first came across the Net in 1991, when I was a low-level worker in an office at Columbia University. My Zappa-look-alike office manager, who already understood cyberdom's awesome potential to slack off on the clock, was obsessed with taking our admissions office online. I saved on long distance by e-mailing my girlfriend, then a grad student at Berkeley, and a few other pioneers

I knew who were connected. But since almost no one had Internet access at the time, for the most part it was like plugging a phone into a rock.

By early 1995, things had changed. I carefully read my fellow cartoonists' work in the daily and weekly press. I noticed that the hipper, cooler, post–"Family Circus" contingent of cartoonists, like Scott Adams ("Dilbert") and Tom Tomorrow ("This Modern World"), listed e-mail addresses next to their signatures.

I assumed that this fad was just the equivalent of CB radio and quadraphonic stereo until I met Tom Tomorrow (actually, his name is Dan Perkins) at a San Francisco bar.

"So, Dan—you don't really hear from that many people, do you?"

"Not that many—I've only got a mailing list of eight hundred."

Eight *hundred*?

One of the most frustrating aspects of cartooning is the profession's pervasive sense of isolation. My cartoons go out every week to more than a hundred publications. Intellectually I know that tens of millions of people read them, but you'd never know it from my regular snail mail. People are too lazy to write.

I don't know why the art of letter writing died, but I stopped trying to generate massive piles of hate mail years ago. The haters never cooperate. In five years of syndication, I've received perhaps two hundred letters

business standpoint, it puts me in touch with people who might be interested in buying my books.

Dan sends periodic e-mail newsletters about his new books, tours, and other Tom Tomorrow–related activities to the people he meets online. Never one to let a bandwagon leave town without me, I called my computer-literate friends to ask which online provider to use. I was about to go

from fans and Bible-thumpers, which averages out to about one letter per five cartoons. (This doesn't include a few notable exceptions—like a piece I did comparing California's Proposition 187 to the Nuremburg laws—that resulted in sacks of mail calling me a "spic-lover.")

It's terribly depressing to create cartoons that seem to vanish into the Delta quadrant. Artistically, I relish reader feedback because it tells me which cartoons affect people. From a

with a local, independent direct-Internet company when another cartoonist friend, Ruben ("Tom the Dancing Bug") Bolling, advised me that AOL gives free accounts to cartoonists in exchange for listing their e-mail addresses on their cartoons. I called around, but none of the smaller, direct-access companies would comp me an account. I'm cheap. I called.

First they sent me the installation disk for DOS. (Owing to my wife's stubborn streak, we have a Mac.) When the Mac disk came, it took three hours to connect to AOL. I called their 800 number for help—the wait was forty-five minutes—only to be told that my "node" was having problems. What about another node? I'd have to wait for my node to be fixed. When would that be? And what exactly *is* a node? It sounds vaguely obscene.

Anyway, my node hadn't been scheduled for repair; more complaints would have to

I eventually logged on, only to be bumped off when someone called in on the other line, activating my call-waiting. It took me weeks of getting bumped before someone told me about blocking call-waiting. (The prefix is *67 in California. When I moved to New York, this didn't work. It's *70 in New York. Because the East Coast is closer to the sun, you add three.)

Now I use several Internet providers, including AOL and Mindspring. No matter

come in. I called four times (to increase the number of complaints). Finally, I got a guy who sounded intelligent enough to tie his shoelaces in the morning. He told me about AOLNet, which allowed me to connect through a less-used, better, faster node.

An entire day closer to death, and I had yet to enter the wonderful world of the Information Superhighway. But I had found my node. The worst of my troubles should have been over.

which service you use, getting online is a major pain in the ass. First you have to keep retrying to get past the busy signals. Half the time, you connect successfully but your connection "times out," whatever that means. Often, for no apparent reason, you're arbitrarily disconnected from the service, usually when you're doing something important or difficult. Either that, or the screen freezes up, forcing you to kill the power and reboot your computer.

Then you have to wait a minute or two—which seems like an eternity in online time—while useless graphics are downloaded. The worst is when the graphics are for advertisers.

You don't have a choice. I don't pay for any online services, yet I still feel ripped off. It took many, many hours of waiting on hold with AOL's help dudes to determine that my modem, the Global Village TelePort Gold II, is an obscure item apparently peddled by itinerant Nepalese merchants.

Accordingly, it requires a customized setup code containing such obvious characters as "78U#%KT400@'L~" to operate.

One might wonder why Internet service providers don't simply publish a booklet addressing every conceivable problem, but this isn't the way the computer industry operates. Instead, their instruction manuals contain *no useful information whatsoever*. Instead, you're expected to call whenever you run into trouble.

Admittedly, the Net is great to search for

old news stories, or to find pictures of cows or Chuck Norris (you wouldn't believe how hard it is to find a picture of either in a standard desk reference), as well as to spend endless hours in chat rooms talking to fifteen-year-old truants about contemporary political issues. I derived great insight into the American character from such online refuse as:

TedRall: Has anyone heard about Newt Gingrich's new school voucher plan?
PrtyGrl87: I'm in KANSAS!!!!!!!!

YurtlDood: MEEEEEEEEEOOOOOO OOOOOWWWWWWWWWW!
BrylnkQ: Yo cat boy shut the fuck up!
PrtyGrl87: Yur> Meow!
YurtlDood: EEEEEEEEEEEEEEEEEEEE EEEEEEEEEEEEEEEEEEEEEEEEEE
TedRall: C'mon, people. This is the News Room. What about vouchers?
John88834: Ted Rall> I'm with Gingrich all the way! Newt ROCKS!
BrlnkQ: CAT MOTHERFUCKER! I got your address (1221 Fleer Ave., Tucson

AZ) from Online Profile and I'm coming to FUCK UP your ass!

During the summer of 1995, I began reading about the World Wide Web, where all good cyberthings supposedly were to be found. When I went to the Web screen under "Internet Connection," I learned that my reliable old AOL Installer for Mac 2.5 was already obsolete. To access the Web, I would need the vastly improved AOL Installer for Mac 2.6, which I promptly downloaded from AOL (time required: thirty-seven minutes). Since then I've been through versions 2.7 and 3.0, each one larger and longer to download. Now you need a computer with sixteen megabytes of RAM just to run AOL 3.0, all because of moving logos and higher-resolution graphics.

Obviously, it would take considerably more than AOL Installer for Mac 2.6 to gain access to the Wonderful World of the

World Wide Web—much, much more.

The first time I clicked on the World Wide Web icon, nothing much happened. A forty-five minute call to AOL's help line later, I reset the Control Panels feature on my Mac. Still no good. Another forty-five minutes. (In the old Richard Pryor skit, everything cost ten bucks. Online, everything takes forty-five minutes.) In accordance with the help line guy, to whom I talked more often in a week than to my mother in a year, I cleaned up my desktop. No go. Yet another forty-five minutes. I was told to take my Web Cache to the trash. I did. Nothing happened, so I went to bed. I'd spent an entire Saturday from 1:00 P.M. to 1:00 A.M. trying to get into the Web. I'm just that kind of person: determined, persevering . . . dumb.

The next day, I logged on, went to the Web icon, and . . . guess what? You'll never believe this. No, you will: It still didn't work. But several weeks later, it did, due to the

stronger pull of gravity during the month of August.

I was fortunate enough to read about the Alta Vista and Lycos Web search tools in the newspaper. If the newspaper weren't there to teach me about the technology destined to replace it, I don't know what I'd do. My first task: locate a picture of Chuck Norris to use in a cartoon. A minute later, I'm staring at three color photos of the *Invasion U.S.A.* star.

I ran my e-mail address for two months on my cartoons before anyone noticed. Messages started trickling in—usually fan mail. I started building up a fan mailing list, which now contains some two thousand e-mail addresses. When my last book came out, I followed Dan's example and sent out a blanket mailing. A few sourpusses sent back surly "Please take me off your mailing list" messages (you know who you are, Garry Trudeau!), but many people requested ordering information. I know that e-mail has been responsible for increasing my book sales.

More important, it's now easy for prospective employers to find me for freelance work. In the past, I had to hope that an art director who liked my style would know that Universal Press Syndicate, my employer, was located in Kansas City, so that he or she could call information for their number. Now, anyone who feels the urge can simply e-mail me, and they do.

Of course, if would-be writers weren't too damn lazy to put thirty-two cents on an envelope, they could write to me in care of the newspapers where my cartoons appear, but in the information age, that's too primitive. It's pretty ironic, when you consider how long it takes to log on and send electronic mail, not to mention the $20-per-month expense.

I think that the real reason people prefer to send e-mail rather than write letters—when the total effort is exactly the same, if not more—is the Net's cachet. The media has convinced America that having your own Web site is the ultimate in cool. Everyone who's anyone is online, goes the thinking, although fewer than 20 percent of Americans really are.

Moreover, you need an e-mail address for your business card, and not just any e-mail address. AOL is the Chrysler K-Car of Internet providers—second-rate, generic. The ultra-chic of the ultra-geeky insist on an address from a local Internet service provider, like the Well in San Francisco or Echo in New York. AOL has added some hip cachet with new content, but cyberpioneers still look down on it. If you're scamming service for free by hacking into the system, that's even cooler than your own column in *Wired*. You have electronic street cred. But

the ultimate test of character in a faceless world of nodes and fictional profiles is possessing your own domain, so that you can customize your e-mail address: ted@rall.com.

Who cares about all this? Not me, but the urge to rush headfirst into modernity is upon us. The Net is the Next Big Thing, and cyberspace is like the land rush of the late 1800s. On the other hand, those aged pundits who claim the Net is the CB radio of the nineties are obviously wrong. Being able to e-mail a picture or an article in a few seconds—for free—renders FedEx's "absolutely overnight, guaranteed" as quaint and antiquated as quill pens.

Like a bachelor's degree, the Net is a filter. People don't have time to ask you the right questions to see if you're smart, so they rely on social symbols of viability. If you have a BA and an e-mail address, you're someone worth talking to. If you're not online, you're offline. Nonexistent scum. Out of the loop.

Although the Internet makes some things more difficult, never underestimate the power of the magical. For instance, people are impressed when I tell them that I transmit my cartoons to my syndicate by posting them to an electronic bulletin board. I don't tell them that I have to tie up my phone line for more than two hours a week when it used to take me five minutes at Kinko's to send them in by FedEx. That would be bad form. Even so, I'm amazed that such big pictures can go through such tiny lines.

A *Village Voice* writer noted that Californians, prone to New Ageism, view the Net as a vehicle of change to create the New Man—spiritual, technological, transcendent. New Yorkers, he says, view it as another business tool, like the laptop and the fax machine. I fit the New York model. I use it because I have to, because it adds to my income by making me more accessible to people who want to hire me, and it puts me in touch with like-minded souls. E-mail is less intrusive than the phone and more effective than a letter.

Still, it's only good sense to be deeply suspicious of an information medium that, taken to its logical extreme, would lead to everyone in the United States sitting on their asses staring at a bluish blinking screen, transacting every bit of business from shopping to dating over lines installed by the federal government's military complex. As for the zombie-citizens in the twenty-four-hour soap operas that use up people's wall space in the post-literature nightmare of *Fahrenheit 451*, the electronic community isn't so much a new form of society as a death knell for an America in which people know their neighbors, their coworkers, and their leaders.

Nonetheless, those who choose to ignore the new technology risk losing opportunities to those who familiarize themselves with it. That's the biggest reason I hate the Net: It's a rare exception to my stubbornness. It's turned me into a conformist—and, God help me, I think I like it.

23. BRING ON THE STOCK MARKET CRASH

"You're either inside or you're outside."
—*Michael Douglas,* Wall Street

Whenever the nation's financial markets go off on a wild roller-coaster ride, as they must every so often, many analysts begin wondering whether the nineties bull market is finally about to grind to a brutal halt, bringing capitalism to an end once and for all, or at least for a while. Jittery mutual fund and institutional investors begin withdrawing their holdings, a habit that only serves to make the next crash even worse, and suddenly the boom-and-bust cycle of the free market starts to look a little less than magical.

So, has the economy really become crash-proof, as the nation's business writers and department-store stockbrokers would have us believe? Or will the market eventually collapse, as it always has in the past? Believe it or not, a lot of people are looking forward to a crash.

The most recent Wall Street crash, in October 1987, had a number of positive results. First, urban property values were decimated, allowing twentysomethings to consider buying homes for the first time. In New York City, for instance, from 1987 to 1991, the average sale price of a new home plunged by more than two-thirds. During the 1980s, Baby Boomer–driven real estate speculation drove up the age of a typical American homebuyer from twenty-four to thirty-two. Now that the trend has reversed, the American dream of home ownership is again within reach of young adults.

The implosion of the real estate market

also caused rents to slump from the absurdly inflated levels of the mid-1980s. In 1988, I was lucky to find a two-bedroom apartment in Spanish Harlem for $1,450 a month; by 1991, my rent could have legally increased to $1,720 under the city's rent stabilization laws, but my landlord considered himself lucky to get $1,200.

During the 1990s, the runaway stock market has driven another round of real estate speculation that has put thousands of people on the streets and squeezed wallets all over the country. Another market correction is long overdue to restore sanity to rents.

If you read *Business Week* or *Forbes,* it's easy to forget that the majority of Americans are renters, not owners. Even for those who are wealthy enough to own their own homes—and make no mistake, owning a house indicates that one enjoys a relatively substantial amount of wealth—a drop in property value is no big deal. It's a paper loss, one that only affects you when you want to sell. As long as you're willing to stay put, you'll still have a place to live. In addition, there's always the option of refinancing at the new lower interest rates that invariably result from cyclical downturns.

Another social advantage of stock market crashes is their leveling effect. Our economy is transforming from a ladder of different income class levels into a two-tiered income structure. According to the *United Nations Human Development Report 1996,* 358 billionaires control wealth greater than the combined annual incomes of countries that have 45 percent of the world's population. Meanwhile, three billion people make less than two dollars a day. As report coauthor James Gustave Speth says, "An emerging global

elite, mostly urban-based and interconnected in a variety of ways, is amassing great wealth and power, while more than half of humanity is left out." Here in the United States, 20 percent of workers earn an average income of $5,814 per annum.

Contrary to corporate propaganda, most Americans don't own stocks. Over 80 percent of stocks, bonds, and options are held by huge institutional investors—the few employees who participate in mutual funds or 401(k)s do not keep a significant percentage of their savings in such securities. When the market crashes, the super-rich suffer, not average citizens. Therefore, in this zero-sum, us-versus-them economy, the super-rich's loss is everyone else's gain.

This is especially true for younger Americans who have either just entered or are preparing to enter the job market. Most wealth is concentrated in the hands of the elderly, who tie it up in stock certificates and

bank CDs. A stock market crash shakes capital loose by bursting the bubble of speculation and forcing the codgers to finally put their cavernous empty-nest three-bedrooms on the market. More directly, older managers and executives are downsized, opening up opportunities for younger workers that otherwise would have not been available.

It is true that, in a recession, layoffs will also hit young, low-level workers. But most layoffs occur in the ranks of middle managers;

the clerical and administrative people do the real work for very little salary, making them far more valuable to their employers. And losing a poorly paying job isn't a big deal—as former middle managers have found since the pit of the recession in 1991, it's a lot harder to replace a six-figure salary with benefits.

Every downturn in the securities markets leads to an avalanche of sad stories about widows whose savings have been wiped out. But we Americans, who have no pity for kids

who sleep in the tub to avoid stray bullets in the projects, certainly shouldn't summon any compassion for someone who got burned by a stock crash. Every investor knows that securities represent a gamble, that higher returns mean greater risk, and that no one should ever invest more than they can afford to lose. Anyone who complains about losing in the market is an insufferable whining fool. Haven't these greedheads ever heard of savings accounts?

Stock market crashes also offer a number of subtler advantages to many Americans, even to those who lose money. The recent "cocooning" trend—in other words, spending quality time with friends and family—is a positive symptom of the desire to put relationships with other people ahead of the pursuit of higher credit limits. That began in the last recession.

But most satisfying of all is the sense crashes provide of mythic retribution against the arrogant rich. Watching the gods of capitalism humbled reminds us of the arbitrary nature of success and the danger of believing your own hype. The further those 358 billionaires fall, the harder I laugh—so bring on the crash!

24. THE END IS HERE

"Oh, well, things crumble to an end
Hell, we all die in the end
Die in the end . . ."
—*Dead Kennedys, "Dead End," 1982*

ive years ago conservative historian Francis Fukuyama argued in his book *The End of History and the Last Man* that the triumph of capitalist democracies over socialism in the Cold War signaled that humanity had evolved to the highest and most fully developed political and economic system imaginable. Events would continue to occur, obviously, but history—the linear progression of Western civilization from ancient dynastic rule to feudalism to industrialization to contemporary society to something new—had ended.

We might devolve into some past form of society, Fukuyama said, but there was nothing new to look forward to. We'd seen it all and done it all, been there, done that. Moreover, we, like Voltaire's Candide, live in this best of all possible worlds.

Similarly, science writer John Horgan wrote a 1996 book, *The End of Science*, that encourages physicists to hang up their Hubble telescopes and get cracking on the mysteries of deep-frying and secret sauce. After all, says Horgan, astronomers and chemists have already described the universe to an enormous extent, from the gravitational interaction of galaxies down to the tiniest subatomic particles. There will be new discoveries, but they'll be tiny little findings—nothing on the order of the Theory of Relativity or anything else that would be worth e-mailing your mom about. "Further research may yield no more great revelations or revolutions, but only incremental, diminishing returns," wrote the undertaker of biology, chemistry, and physics. Science is a wrap. Please take

your personal belongings with you when you leave the room.

Film schools teach their students that there are, and only can be, no more than thirty-six types of stories that can ever be told. Every tale, whether it be by Poe, Tolstoy, or Scorcese, is by necessity a variation on one of those thirty-six themes. A logical mind might extrapolate that as there must have once been only thirty-five stories, there should be a thirty-seventh story lurking in one of the 6 billion minds running around

out there, but devotees of screenwriting theory are adamantly opposed to this prospect.

Rock critics write that there are no new songs to be written, just rehashes of old ones—thus, rock too is dead. Mediocre painters and architects interpret their own lack of new ideas as proof that there are no new ones to be found. Yup, art is dead, architecture is dead, everything is dead, dead, dead.

What an utter load of dung.

Throughout history moribund societies have always believed that they had developed

THE LONG KISS GOODNIGHT
Your Final Guide to What's Over, Finished, Kaput, and Dead as a Doornail

IT'S	WHUZZUP?	DO YOU CARE?
The End of Arachnids!	Eventually all spiders and scorpions could die off, but no one has actually said that this will happen.	Sure, if you own real estate in New Mexico or Arizona.
The End of Books!	Books are being replaced by the Internet; in the future everyone will take their laptops to the beach.	Yeah, right. As if!
The End of Cars!	We'll run out of oil in 50 to 100 years; since big oil companies won't allow electric cars, everyone will end up walking or taking the bus or subway.	See The End of Subways.
The End of Comedy!	Soon irony, detached alienation, and the current taboo against making fun of other people will make it impossible to get a laugh.	If you'd miss comedy, no one will miss you.
The End of Eating Out!	You'll soon be able to order food online, and longer work weeks will make it impossible for workers to get out at night.	Only if you own a restaurant or enjoy watching other people yell at their kids in public.
The End of Friendship!	See The End of Eating Out.	No biggie—we've still got television!
The End of Frogs!	*The New York Times Magazine* once devoted an entire issue to the question of whether pollution is killing off the world's frog population.	Pollution is killing you, too—let the little green guys fend for themselves.
The End of Money!	Debit cards, credit cards, automatic toll collection devices, and automatic payment deductions from your bank account will eventually make cash obsolete.	How the hell are we supposed to rob banks if they don't have any money?
The End of Music!	Record companies are bleeding because they've created so many musical genres that it's impossible for any single artist to have a hit anymore.	This, of course, means the end of Michael Bolton. Draw your own conclusions.

IT'S	WHUZZUP?	DO YOU CARE?
The End of Nations!	Free-trade agreements, the rise of the European Union, and the collapse of protectionism in Asia are eroding national sovereignty.	If you can't understand the news, it can't hurt you.
The End of Parenthood!	If you hit your child he'll call the cops. You can't care for him because you work two jobs. People are having kids later—even when they are no longer fertile.	Losing that tax deduction hurts, but think of all the college tuition you'll eventually save.
The End of Peace!	The dominant trend in global politics is balkanization; eventually every tiny clan will insist on its own country, which will lead to endless war.	Only if you lose your little war.
The End of Psychotherapy!	Americans are turning away from their shrinks in record numbers: Why pay $150 an hour for advice you can get for free on the radio?	Nope.
The End of Sitcoms!	Every possible fish-outta-water scenario has already been done; in a world in which *Three's Company* meets *Hill Street Blues* (in *NYPD Blue*), is there anywhere else to go?	The end of the sitcom could lead to the end of network TV, which could lead to the end of network TV news, which could make Ted Turner even wealthier than he is now.
The End of Suburbia!	The suburbs are crowded, crime-ridden, and decadent; people are either moving back to the inner cities or out to the countryside.	When the 'burbs become slums, are they still 'burbs or are they slurbs?
The End of Subways!	It now costs $2 billion to dig one mile of subway line in New York City, making it unlikely that anyone will ever build one again.	Not if you own stock in oil companies.
The End of War!	When everyone from France to the Falklands has nukes, no one can really afford to start a war.	See The End of Peace.
The End of Winter!	Global warming has eliminated snow from most American cities.	At last—the Endless Summer goes national!
The End of You!	Everything that you know and love and hate is gone . . . so who needs you?	Depends on which "you" you're talking about.

the ultimate art, political system, or technology. Every new regime has considered its own to be the logical—and final—culmination of everything that had come before it. They couldn't imagine a different world, so they denied that change was possible. And here we go again.

If history is really over, why try to make society more egalitarian? After all, we already know the option of socialism is a washout. Einstein proved that travel faster than the speed of light is impossible, so give up those romantic dreams of flying off to some dis-

tant star. If painters really have nothing new to say, why bother with those messy oils? Human existence becomes predicated on the base struggle for day-to-day survival.

Given the track record of Hitler's "Thousand-Year Reich," Khrushchev's assertion that he'd bury the United States, and the music industry executives who thought rap would never catch on, we should know by now to always expect the unexpected. Instead, our shortsightedness is matched only by our arrogance.

The Fukuyama-Horgan school of developmental finality is especially disturbing for the inevitable corollary to its millenarian "that's all, folks" thesis: that there's no point in even trying to accomplish, see, or experience anything new. We might as well kill all of our children, since they'll know all of life's warmed-over misery and none of its joy of discovery.

We know that there must be millions of new ideas, some waiting to be stumbled upon and others already around and understood by a few but unnoticed by the world at large—for now. For instance, physicists now believe space can be folded over itself to create wormholes—allowing faster-than-light travel and proving Einstein wrong.

There have to be new things to discover, otherwise we'd never get up in the morning. Those of us who know that we'll never have all the answers ought to recognize those who say different as the irrelevant, exhausted wrecks that they are. And just because they have abandoned their own imaginations doesn't mean the rest of us should do the same.

And fast on the heels of sheep cloning, geneticists have discovered how to clone a person who died decades ago from a tissue sample—the scenario predicted in *The Boys from Brazil*. Some call it the end of evolution, but it's really something new: self-evolution, by which people will self-select which DNA strands get to move on to the next generation. While this technology offers endless possibilities for corruption, it might also permit humanity to determine its destiny. No, wait, that can't be! After all, everything's done, everywhere's the same, and everyone's dead.